How to Write Small Reports and Get Paid

A Step-By-Step System For Writing And Profiting From 7-15 Page Reports

By

Todd Ramse

How to Write Small Reports and Get Paid

Welcome to How to *"Write Small Reports and Get Paid"*™ where I'm going to teach you "write small reports and earn money doing so".

We'll talk at length about how to do this, but I want to kind of encapsulate everything into one opening statement as we begin our presentation –

The ultimate information business is finding a target audience
and then convincing them to make repeated purchases from you.

An age-old marketing law is this: *"it's much easier to sell MORE to existing customers than it is to find new customers to sell to".* Your information business stands to gain serious momentum when you offer multiple, related offers to your customer base.

Instead of selling a customer a $20 ebook and then looking for the next customer, you'll want to setup a system to offer her a $20 ebook, then a $40 product, then a $497 product and finally a $1997 offer. (These are just "generalities", of course.)

And it's all going to build upon this foundation of creating short, 7-15 page reports.

The important thing is to get your existing customers to spend MORE money with you. Learn this: the more money each customer spends with you, the less customers you'll need to reach $100K per year, or possibly much more.

<u>The idea is simple</u>: get your target audience (subscribers + customers) to repeatedly spend money with you.

> ***Once you have worked to secure a customer or subscriber, why not***
> ***allow them to spend as much money with you as they are willing?***

I'm not suggesting that you exploit your relationship with others and coerce them into purchasing sub-par products or things they don't really have a need to buy. I'm talking about making products and services available that provide genuine usefulness to those who are in a position to buy.

There's a big, big difference between these two statements:

> *"This product is going to change your business forever ... it's the best product I've seen in months ... if you don't buy this today, then you're absolutely nuts ... it's what I consider to be a 'must-have' for anyone who's serious!"*

> *"If you're ready to XYZ, then I've found this product to be very beneficial in my own business. I use it myself and here are the results that I've achieved. I highly recommend it and will even give you a free copy of XYZ if you are one of the first 50 who buy it."*

Both are attempting to get the sale. *But one is full of hype and the other is reasonable.*

Back to my point. You need to get your target audience to buy from you. And buy again. And again. And again.

Despite popular belief, you can do this without being a money-hungry, conscious-less, in-your-face, psychological mind-games coercer. (That's a mouthful, huh?!)

So, that's the backdrop of this course. I'm going to teach you how to -

CHOOSE a market, *CREATE* small reports to sell to them
and *CASH-IN* on your own money-making information business.

What I want to teach you to do in this series is to **create small, 7-15 page reports that you sell to your list members in the $10-$20 range**...and how to spiral them into premium-priced offers down the road.

You can make a "small fortune" with "small reports" - and I'm going to show you how to do it.

Here's what it looks like 12 months from now:

You have 12 reports available for $10 each.
(One per month)

Customers buy the first one and, in time, buy most of

the others.
(Multiple customer purchases)

You put together package deals of 12 reports for $97.
(Larger chunks of cash per transaction)

You launch an affiliate program for the $97 package
and sell large quantities of the bundle.
(Affiliates love ~$50 commission per order!)

You use your reports to launch "high ticket"
offers that sell for $1,000 or more. (Skyrocket your
profit!)

You make a "small fortune" with "small reports"
(Yes, YOU!)

And it all begins right here.

So, we need to talk about choosing a "market" that
you want to build your business around. A "market" is
simply a broad, general topic such as "weight loss",
"home business" and "relationships" to name a few.

You might look at it in terms of a "target audience":
the people who are interested in a "market" such as
"those wanting to lose weight", "those wanting to start
and grow a home business" and "those wanting to
have healthy relationships".

The important thing is to choose something "broad"
and not a "niche". The reason for this is simple:

**_You want to create multiple, related reports
to offer your target audience._**

What you want to do is determine what "market" is best for you as you begin creating these small reports.

3 Simple Rules For Choosing A Market

Now, for me, I have three simple criteria that I look at in deciding what I want to focus upon. I'd suggest that you do the same in evaluating what market you want to build your business upon.

1. A market accustomed to spending money.

If the market isn't accustomed to spending money – and, generally, a "*lot*" of money, then there's no point in directing any effort towards it. "*College students*" isn't a great target audience simply because most of them are broke! On the other hand, "*golfers*" spend a gazillion dollars each year on their hobby … they certainly would qualify.

2. A market that can be presented with a wide variety of offers.

If the market is limited in what you can sell to it, then again there is a red flag. You want to be able to present multiple offers related to the general theme of the target audience you have selected.

Let's take the example of the weight loss market. You can sell a variety of both digital and physical products to this market, including:

- Reports, ebooks, access to membership sites, videos and live events on a wide variety of topics, including nutrition, strength training, cardio exercise, supplements, motivation and more.
- Physical products such as vitamins, diet supplements, pre-packaged food items, exercise equipment and similar merchandise.
- Coaching, consulting and other services such as nutrition counseling, personal training and similar services.

Point is, the people in this market don't just buy one item and call it a day. Instead, they are receptive to a wide variety of products and services, and many people in the market will buy multiple related products and services over their lifetime. (And, as you'll find out later in this guide, you'll be selling a variety of these offers to your existing customers to build your business!)

3. A market that you are personally attracted to. (Optional)

While this isn't absolutely necessary, it's certainly a plus. If you can find a target audience / market that meets points 1 and 2 - AND you have a strong

interest in it yourself, then you've made
your choice.

A personal interest, experience or
knowledge of a particular target audience
gives you an advantage in many areas of
building your business. It's not
necessary, but it does help.

Now, having said that, you **need to pick a market**. I'm including a list of over 60 major markets that I encourage you to choose from in making your selection.

Index of Profitable Markets

* Listed alphabetically

Markets

- Aging / Senior Interests
- Antiques And Collectibles
- Arts And Crafts
- Automotive
- Baby And Child
- Beauty (Skincare / Haircare)
- Business (Auctions)
- Business (General)
- Business (Internet)
- Business (Opportunities)
- Business (Small / Home)
- Cancer Survival /
- Investing And Finance
- Kids And Teens
- Leadership
- Men's Issues
- Motivational
- Non-Profit And Fundraising
- Outdoors
- Parenting
- Pets
- Photography
- Public Speaking
- Real Estate
- Recreation And Sports
- Relationships

- Support
- Career And Jobs
- Coaching And Consulting
- Communication
- Computer (Hardware)
- Computer (Software)
- Computers And Technology
- Consumer Protection
- Cooking
- Dating
- Disease And Illness
- Education
- Fashion
- Finance And Investment
- Health And Fitness
- Hobbies
- Home And Family
- Home Repair / Improvement
- Home Schooling
- Interior Decorating
- Internet
- Religion (Christianity)
- Retirement
- Retail Businesses
- Romance
- Sales And Marketing
- Success
- Self Improvement / Help
- Sexuality
- Shopping
- Sports (Golf, Tennis, Etc.)
- Stock Market
- Time Management
- Travel And Leisure
- Wedding And Marriage
- Wellness And Remedies
- Women's Issues
- Writing

Now, as you think about what market you'd like to enter, consider these two additional tips:

Tip #1: Choose an evergreen market.

This is a market that is relevant today, it was relevant last year, and it will be relevant (and popular) two years from now. As you can see, the above markets are all evergreen – they don't go "stale." This gives you the opportunity to keep selling to the same market for years to come.

> Example: example of NON-evergreen markets include creating information around something that's new and likely to fall out of favor, such as a specific MLM opportunity or a controversial diet that has just entered the market. While the overall markets are evergreen (the business market and the weight-loss market), the topics or niche markets are not evergreen.

So, in sum, ask yourself if the market has been around for a long time… and if it's likely to continue to be around for some time to come.

> Extra Tip: Need a little help with this step? Then check out Google Trends at http://www.google.com/trends/. This site gives you a snapshot look at how popular a topic is over several years, which gives you an indication of whether it's an evergreen topic. But best of all, it also shows you which direction the topic is trending. If you see your topic has been trending upwards for a few years, that's a great sign.

Tip #2: Choose a big and profitable market.

In other words, choose a market with a lot of people buying products and services, and a lot of marketers servicing these people. This shows you that the market is big, healthy and profitable.

The way you can determine if a market is big is simply by doing a little research online and offline. Run a search in Amazon as well as Google for the market's main keywords (such as "European travel" or "weight loss"), and then ask yourself these questions:

- **Are their local shops and service providers catering to this market?** For example, if you run a search for weight loss, you'll find local gyms, personal trainers, nutritionists, exercise supply stores, vitamin and supplement supply stores and similar commercial enterprises all selling their products and services offline. The reason this is important is because you want to make sure the market is so big that it's not just confined to internet users.

- **Are there plenty of different products and services being sold on the market?** This goes back to my point above that you want to find a market that is receptive to a wide variety of offers.

- **Is there a lot of competition?** This is actually a good thing, as it shows you that the market is healthy.

- **Are marketers paying to reach this market?** Are they placing paid ads in offline publications as well as on websites (such as banner ads or the sponsored listings in search engines)? Again, these are all good signs of a healthy market, as no one spends money if they aren't making back this investment.

You'll want to pick a market where you get a resounding "yes" to each of the above questions.

Another way to get a sense of the size of the market is to use a keyword tool like WordTracker.com (or even Google's Keyword tool). What you do is enter in your market's broad keywords (like "weight loss"), and the tool will show you how many times that particular keyword is searched. You're looking for big markets where the big keywords are searched into the six figures every month (e.g., 100,000+).

> Note: Another way to get a feel for the size of a market is to use Facebook's advertising tools at https://www.facebook.com/advertising. If you log into Facebook and pretend like you're going to set up an ad, Facebook will tell you how many people on their network you'll be able to reach by searching for specific user interests.

Now, once you use all the tips above, it will become fairly clear which markets are big and profitable. Then you need to choose one. If it's clear that one of your markets looks bigger and more profitable than the other ones on your list, that's the one you can choose. If you're not sure which is the biggest or most profitable, no problem: pick the one that interests you the most.

Generally, if you pick a market from the list above or one that's closely related, then you already know it's a big, profitable and evergreen market.

After you've determined to which market you're going to sell your small reports, it's time to get into the actual process of creating and profiting from those reports.

In the coming sections of this course, we're going to cover everything you need to get this end result...

Section #1: How To Find The Perfect Idea For A Small Report.

Section #2: How To Write P.A.G.E.S. Of High Demand Content.

Section #3: How To Package, Price and Position Your Small Report.

Section #4: How To Create A Small Report Mini-Sales letter.

Section #5: How To S.E.T.U.P. A Web Site To Sell Your Small Report

Section #6: How To Turn Small Reports Into A Six-Figure Business

This is going to be a dynamic presentation that will really help you create extra income for your business.

Let's go ahead and begin...

How To Find The Perfect Idea For A Small Report

In our first section we're going to examine, "*How To Find the Perfect Idea For A Small Report*".

Now before we look at the two basic rules of thought about finding hot ideas that I want to share with you today, let me first caution you about a potential problem area that might sidetrack you if you're not prepared.

Let me say it this way -

Don't invest a <u>lot</u> of time in
choosing a topic for your small report.

That's <u>not</u> to say that you should make an **uninformed decision** as to what you should write about. To the contrary, I'm going to show you how to determine with ***pinpoint accuracy*** what is most likely to be a hot seller for you.

<u>What I am saying is this</u>: this is a SMALL report. It's not a full-length product. It isn't necessary that you spend a great deal of time trying to find the ideal subject matter. You're not trying to hit a home run here. You're not trying to write the equivalent of *War and Peace* for your particular market. You're simply looking for an idea that looks to be a winner to write a short report about.

Don't miss the point here. The point is to QUICKLY create these small reports.

There's not much risk here. So there's not much point in over-investing your time in any stage of this process.

Now, having said all of that, let's look at two criteria that I believe will allow you to quickly analyze the state of your market interest and ascertain what should prove to be a hot topic for your next small report.

CRITERIA 01: **Demand.** That is, there should be a significant amount of interest in a particular idea before you move forward. Obviously, the more interest there is in a topic, the more likely you'll be able to sell a report on that topic.

Now, the questions that I almost always get from folks are -

How can I judge "demand" or "interest" towards a particular idea?

How can I find ideas that are in "demand"?

There are a number of ways to find topics that are of significant demand and interest to your marketplace. Very quickly let me share <u>eight ways</u> you can find topics that are "making a splash" within your particular market.

1. **Keep an eye out on Clickbank's Marketplace**. Products that range in the top 5 positions within a particular category are usually selling very well. I'll give you a quick hint: they wouldn't be selling well if there wasn't interest. :-) Look for categories in the marketplace that

are related to your particular target audience and scan through the top 5-6 products listed. You're certain to find some great ideas for your small report right there. (And you might even find a great product to promote as your "backend" - more on this in a future lesson). Clickbank's Marketplace can be found at http://www.clickbank.com/marketplace

> Example: Put in the broad keyword "weight loss," and then take note of the results that show up at the top of the list – these are your most popular products (your bestsellers). You'll likely see books on topics such as getting rid of belly fat, using weight training to get slim and using special kinds of diets to lose weight, such as Paleo diets and vegetarian diets.

In addition to taking note of your bestsellers, you'll also want to look for patterns that indicate a particular topic is popular with the market.

> Example: If you see several similar books on the exact same topic on the first page or so of results, that's a good indicator that the topic is in-demand. In the case of weight loss, for example, you might see several books on the topic of getting rid of belly fat.

2. **Scan the best-sellers list as Amazon.com.** Do a search at Amazon.com (in the "books" section) for keywords and phrases that are

related to your particular market. (I.E. "weight loss" or "homeschooling" or "golf") You should find a nice list of books ranked in order of popularity. This is another built-in research spot for you - and loaded with great ideas for your next small report.

You do the same thing here as you did in the Clickbank marketplace. Specifically:

> 1. Pay attention to the bestsellers appearing at the top of your search results.
>
> 2. Look for multiple books on the same topic, which demonstrates demand for that topic.

3. Search in Google.com to see what topics your "competition" has created products on. Pay attention to those listed on the first page and those who are advertising in the ads on the right hand side of the screen. These will almost always provide you with numerous ideas for your small report - and can potentially be a great starting point for joint venture partnerships in the future. (More on this in an upcoming lesson).

To get a really good idea of what your prospective competitors are selling, you can search for a range of related keywords.

> Example #1: Let's suppose you're looking for weight loss sites. Your broad searches might include:

- Weight loss
- Losing weight
- Losing fat
- Fat loss
- Dieting

Example #2: or let's suppose your broad market is golf. You might search for:

- Golf
- Golf tips
- Golf swing
- Golf secrets

You get the idea – expand your search a bit with related keywords, and you'll get a better overview of what your competitors are selling.

4. **Look in the market-related forums for "Hot-Topics" that might lend themselves to report ideas**. There are forums (Aka "message boards") for just about every market imaginable. Look for discussions at these forums for ideas. Specifically, look for topics where there is a LOT of discussion (I.E. Numerous posted messages and replies). Pay special attention for people who are complaining about problems or limitations that you might be able to provide solutions for in your small report.

Also, take note that some forums have "keyword clouds" which show you which keywords are most popular on the forum. This too will give you an idea of what topics your market wants to know more about.

To find forums in your market, search for your keywords (such as "weight loss" or "lose weight" or "dieting") alongside forum related words such as "forum," or "discussion forum" or "message board."

Examples:

- Dieting forum
- Weight loss message board
- Weight loss discussion

5. **Look in popular article directories for existing interest**. Drop by article banks such as GoArticles.com, or EzineArticles.com and look at articles related to your market for brainstorming ideas. Pay special attention to the "most viewed" articles as they are a good indicator of which topics are hot and which topics are not. Also, take note of topics that pop up repeatedly and have high views, as this gives an indication of which topics are most popular.

6. **Find offline magazines related to your market**. Drop by your favorite bookstore or newsstand (or visit Magazines.com online) and look at their articles for small report ideas. In particular, pay attention to the articles appearing on the front cover of these magazines, as those are the topics the publishers expect to garner the most interest.

This is another tremendous way to find great ideas - especially because you get the benefit of THEIR research. They've already invested time in deciding WHAT to write about based on their market's interest. You don't need to do this kind of research... simply write about what they are writing about!

7. **Ask subscribers on a mailing list in your market (either your own opt-in list or one that you rent) which topics interest them most**.

    It's a simple process:

    a. Ask your list members what topics interest them the most.

    b. Take the topic that gets the most mentions and write your small report about it.

    Who better to give you ideas about what to write than those who are most likely to buy the small report upon its completion?

8. **See what's popular on Facebook**. This social media platform gives users the ability to set up groups and pages which revolve around specific interests.

    All you have to do to find them is log into Facebook and run a search for your broad keywords on the upper left side of your screen. From there you can browse the pages and groups to see what they're selling and which topics garner the most "likes," "shares" and discussion.

So, there are eight "interest indicators" that will allow you to quickly judge demand for an idea before you write about it. By using these simple techniques, you should be able to brainstorm quite a few great ideas for your report.

And once you have, let me address the second "criteria" for a hot-selling small report...

CRITERIA 02: **Distinctness.** That is, there needs to be something very SPECIFIC and DEFINITE about your small report that makes it appealing to your marketplace. The more precise you can be in your focus, the more likely it will be a hot seller. Remember, these are 7-15 page reports --- you can't possibly create a "tell-all", in-depth manual on a topic in that short space.

You need to finely focus your report on a precise topic.

Now, there are two general ways to go about doing this that I want to mention here which should be very helpful to you...

> Option A: SEGMENTED. That is, you take a smaller, specific section of a larger idea and you explain it in great detail.
>
> -----------
> For example: It's not "*creating information products*", it's "*hiring ghostwriters to create information products*". And you can even narrow that down to "*5 keys to negotiating rock-bottom*

prices for a top-notch ghostwriter".

Let me give you a great hint here: Go to a sales page for an existing product related to your market. Look at their BULLET POINTS (these are benefit statements usually in a list of bullet points) and you should find some great "segments" to focus on.

Let's assume you want to create a small report related to "*selling information products*". If you go to **www.ContentWritingMadeEasy.com**, you'll find the following bullet point: "*How to Write an Ezine Article.*"

That one bullet point is a perfect idea for your next small report. Write a small report that teaches people how to write articles which get published, attract attention, engage readers and get click-throughs and sales. And when you position it (we'll talk about this in an upcoming lesson) properly, it would absolutely sell like crazy.

Option B: SUPPLEMENTED. That is, you create a list of as many different ideas for one topic as you possibly can. Some examples might include...

- 24 ways to get your email messages delivered.
- 17 ways to lose an extra pound of weight.

- 21 ways to cut costs at the gas pump.
- 19 ways to make money selling products on eBay.
- 27 ways to save a marriage that's headed for divorce.

The idea is to give your reader as many possible ideas as you can think of. I've done this numerous times in the past with great success.

People want to know as many different OPTIONS as are available. The thinking is, they can find at least one or two of those ideas to work for them and their situation. When you only share "one" basic operation, many people find themselves thinking, *"That sounds great ... but I don't think I can do it."*

With a wide variety of ideas, almost everyone finds something useful.

If you identify, let's say 20 *"ways"* or *"ideas"* for some particular topic, then you'd only need to write 1/2 page per idea to have a 10-page report. Simple!

With these two "criteria" (demand and distinctness) you should be able to quickly establish some great ideas for your next small report. In fact, you should have a flood of ideas coming in. Spend half an hour brainstorming ideas. That should yield PLENTY of results.

Note: One more quick tip before we close out. Save all of your ideas that you come up with. Create a "swipe file" with them for future use. There's no need to go through this process again in 30 days when you already have the information at your fingertips. Additionally, as you are going through your business routines (you know the drill: reading forum posts, browsing articles, looking over new offers, etc.) record any new great ideas that you see. These will be great options for future small reports.

Note Number Two: Yeah, I know, I say "one" more quick tip. If you don't want to read this one, then skip on down to my closing remarks. :-) For those of you who want to read something beneficial, this one's for you.

When you are developing these reports, think "series". If you can develop a general "theme" or a "title" that can be tweaked and duplicated over time, you should be able to get more customers to buy most (if not ALL) of your future installments.

> Example: those who buy the "Five Minute Guide to Building Affiliate Lists" will likely buy the "Five Minute Guide to Writing Affiliate Ads" and the "Five Minute Guide to Creating Monthly Affiliate Commissions".

There's something magnetic about a "series" of similarly themed or titled reports.

Okay, that's a wrap for this one. Really. This time it is. No more quick tips. :-)

In our next section we'll talk about **turning your idea into information** as we look at how to actually write your small report.

So, let's go ahead and do that now...

How To Write P.A.G.E.S.™ Of High-Demand Content For Your Special Report

In this section, we're going to examine, *"How To Write P.A.G.E.S.™ Of High-Demand Content"*. But, before we begin with that, let me briefly say a word about *"entitling"* your special report.

Learn this from the beginning -

The <u>title</u> of your report plays a huge role in the conversion of browsers into buyers.

In other words, it's important that your title be something more appealing than, *"Todd's Report on Creating Small Reports"*. ☺

While there are numerous criteria that you might want to consider in choosing a title, I've narrowed it down to what I consider to be the three most important considerations. As the cliché' goes, it's as *"easy as A,B,C"*...

> **A. Does the title "<u>A</u>ccurately represent"?** In other words, does your title mention "specifically" what's included in the report? *"How To Vacation"* isn't specific. *"How to Plan a Vacation"* is still too vague. *"How to Plan A Vacation in 3 Easy Steps"* is narrowing it down better. *"Ways To Save Money At The Gas Pump"* isn't nearly as specific as *"21 Ways to Save Money At The Gas Pump"* or *"The Top 7 Ways to Save Money At The Gas Pump"*.

B. Does the title "Build interest"? That is, is your report title "*appealing*", even "*enticing*"? Your title should, in itself, begin to create a desire to purchase the report. "How to Plan a Vacation in 3 Easy Steps" isn't nearly as appealing as "How to Plan a Fun-Filled, Budget-Friendly Vacation in 3 Easy Steps". Of course, that title isn't nearly as intriguing as "How to Take The Vacation Of Your Dreams Without Spending A Penny!" (Which, by the way, I can *literally* tell you how to do, it's a legitimate report ... do you think it has much appeal?!)

C. Does the title "Communicate benefits"? That is, when someone reads the title of your report, do they have a reasonable expectation of some desirable results they can achieve by purchasing, reading and applying your report? Products that scream ULTIMATE BENEFIT are the most appealing, simply because we are emotional creatures. We want something that is going to deliver the desired results we are after. And if a product title communicates that is can deliver those results, we will definitely take a closer look.

"Earn Income On The Web" doesn't offer nearly the benefit punch that "Get Web Profits Fast!" does. Note the difference: One says "income," the other says "profits." We want money we can spend. One says "Earn" and the other says "Get." Earn seems like much more work that getting something. And one doesn't promise when. The other says "Fast!" See the difference?

For special report titles, go by the three considerations that I just gave you. In most cases, a simple *"How To"* title will work best. Occasionally, depending upon what you're writing, what I call a *"numerical"* title will work well: *"21 Ways to Save Money At The Gas Pump"*, *"7 Ways to Legally 'Steal' Your Competitors' Web Site Traffic"* and *"The One Secret Way to Getting Any Woman to Fall In Love With You That Never Fails"* are examples of this kind of title.

20 Title Templates You Can Use Right Now

Now let me share with you 20 specific title templates you can use to create your next report:

1. The Secrets of [Getting a Benefit] in [Number] Easy Steps

Examples:

- The Secrets of Quickly and Easily Losing 10 Pounds in Just Three Easy Steps

- The Secrets of Creating a Backyard Chicken Coop in Just Five Easy Steps

2. How to [Get Benefit] and [Get Benefit] Without [Doing Something Unpleasant or Having Some Prerequisite]

Examples:

- How to Get a Big Promotion and a Pay Raise Without Haggling With Your Boss

- How to Start Up Your Own Successful Online Business Without Investing Any Money

3. The Shocking [Topic] Secret [Some Group] Doesn't Want You to Know

<u>Examples</u>:

- The Shocking Money-Saving Secrets Your Car Dealer Doesn't Want You to Know

- The Shocking Weight-Loss Secret Your Personal Trainers Doesn't Want You to Know

4. The Cold, Hard Truth About [Topic] – And Why [Some Shocking Fact About the Topic]

<u>Examples</u>:

- The Cold, Hard Truth About Losing Weight -- And Why What Your Doctor or Nutritionist Told You May Cause You To Gain 10 Pounds

- The Cold, Hard Truth About Buying a Home – And Why Most New Homeowners Spend Too Much Money When They Could Get the Same House for Less

5. The #1 Way to [Get a Benefit] – Even if [You Don't do Some Specific Thing]

<u>Examples</u>:

- The #1 Way to Land an Exciting and High-Paying Career – Even if You Never Finished College!

- The #1 Way to Lose Weight Quickly and Easily in Just Six Weeks – Even if You Hate Exercising!

6. How to [Get a Benefit] in [Number] Incredibly Simple Steps

Examples:

- How to Grow Trophy-Winning Roses in Three Incredibly Simple Steps

- How to Train a Wild Puppy to Become a Well-Mannered Companion in Five Incredibly Simple Steps

7. What the World's [Best/Top/Strongest/Richest/Etc] [Type of People] Know About [Getting a Benefit]

Examples:

- What's the World's Best Copywriters Know About Writing High-Response Ads and Sales Letters

- What the World's Top Natural Bodybuilders Know About Developing Rock-Hard Abs

8. How to [Get a Benefit] In Just [Length of Time]

Examples:

- How to Get Rid of Belly Fat and Start Turning Heads in just Eight Short Weeks From Now

- How to Pull Out, Disassemble, Tune, Clean and Reassemble Your Classic Mustang's Carburetor In One Quick Afternoon

9. The Quick and Easy Way to [Get a Benefit]

Examples:

- The Quick and Easy Way to Groom Your Poodle to Look Like a Trophy-Winning Show Dog

- The Quick and Easy Way to Add 25 Yards to Your Golf Swing

10. [Number] Red-Hot Secrets for [Getting Some Benefit]

Examples:

- 7 Red-Hot Secrets for Making a Great First Impression With a Potential Employer

- 27 Red-Hot Secrets for Writing Mouthwatering Sales Copy That Converts

11. [Number] Quick and Easy Ways to [Get Some Benefit]

Examples:

- 11 Quick and Easy Ways to Save $1000 on Your Home Heating and Cooling Bills This Year

- 5 Quick and Easy Ways to Lose 10 Pounds Before Summer

12. [Number] Incredibly Powerful Tips for [Getting Some Benefit]

Examples:

- 12 Incredibly Powerful Tips for Saving $1 Million For Your Retirement

- 3 Incredibly Powerful Tips for Getting Rid of Wrinkles and Looking 10 Years Younger

13. [Number] Habits [Which Create Some Good Result]

Examples:

- 7 Surprising Habits of People Who've Lost At Least 50 Pounds

- 5 Powerful Habits of Highly Successful CEOs

14. How [Some Simple Thing] Can [Get Some Great Result]

Examples:

- How a Common Herb in Your Cupboard Can Restore Your Youthful Good Looks and Vitality

- How One Simple Money-Saving Trick Can Create A Comfortable Retirement for You

15. The Art of [Getting Some Benefit]

Examples:

- The Art of Writing High-Response Sales Letters

- The Art of Growing Delicious Tomatoes (Even if You Don't Have a Green Thumb)

16. A Beginner's Guide to [Some Topic or Getting Some Benefit]

Examples:

- The Beginner's Guide to Creating a Resume That Lands You an Interview With Your First-Choice Company

- The Beginner's Guide to Growing Delicious Vegetables in Your Organic Garden

17. What You Always Wanted to Know About [Some Topic]

Examples:

- What You Always Wanted to Know About Deep-Sea Scuba Diving

- What You Always Wanted to Know About Enjoying a Luxury Vacation on a Shoestring Budget

18. How to [Think, Act, Behave or Get Results] Like [Some Type of Expert]

Examples:

- How to Start, Run and Manage a Business Like The World's Highest-Paid CEOs

- How to Get Lean Fast Like a Competitive Bodybuilder

19. The [Number] [Topic] Rules of Every [Type of Person Ought to Know]

Examples:

- The 7 Fat Loss Rules Every Dieter Ought to Know

- The 10 Success Rules Every Aspiring Entrepreneur Ought to Know

20. [Number] Dos and Don'ts for [Getting Some Benefit]

Examples:

- 27 Dos and Don'ts for Successfully Selling Your Own Home for Top Dollar
- 15 Dos and Don'ts for Throwing a Super-Fun Dinner Party That Everyone Will Rave About for Months Afterwards

Okay, so after establishing some criteria for the title of your report, let's talk about content.

Over the years that I've been online, I've written many, many **pages of content** (products, reports, articles, etc.). I have a simple five-step formula that I use for creating lengthier pieces of content (I.E. reports and products) that I've never shared before in the format I'm about to give to you in this lesson.

The system is called "P.A.G.E.S." Each letter (P - A - G - E - S) stands for one of the five steps in the system...

P - PLAN out your report by brainstorming ideas.
A - ARRANGE your ideas sequentially or systematically.

```
G - GROW your content by "filling in the
blanks".
E - EXTRACT bullet points for your ad
copy while you write.
S - SMOOTH out the rough spots to
complete the report.
```

What I'm going to do in the remainder of this session is briefly explain to you how to put each of these five steps - these five parts of the P.A.G.E.S. system - into action so you can quickly and easily create your own 7-15 page reports to sell.

So, let's go ahead and begin with step #1...

Step #1: PLAN out your report by brainstorming ideas.

Obviously, by this time, you should have chosen a topic to build the content of your report around. So, where do you start? You start by simply brainstorming ideas for possible inclusion in your report. The easiest way that I've discovered for doing this is to simply...

Write a list of everything you want to share.

That's right, just write down everything you want to share in your report. I'm talking just start rambling on paper (or your computer screen). Everything you can think of that relates to the subject of your report. Just a list of "ideas" you want to share.

Here's what I want you to understand about writing: writing is...

THINKING ON PAPER.

That's all writing is. It's putting your thoughts down on paper. Or, onto your computer screen. That's all you need to do – write your thoughts down.

Don't worry about relevance or whether or not you'll even use all of these ideas. Just get them down. Think on paper.

Jot down as many of these as you can find...

- Ideas
- Notes
- Lists
- Questions
- Reminders
- Personal reflections
- Thoughts
- Things-To-Do
- Checklists
- Details
- Steps
- Facts
- Reasons
- Comparisons
- Contrasts
- Statistics
- Quotes
- Illustrations / Stories

Write down everything you can think of or find during your research.

Don't worry about whether or not it makes sense. Don't worry about how well it's written. Don't worry about that it doesn't fit with anything else. Just write down everything you can possibly think of concerning the topic of your report.

Now, I want to give you one of the most invaluable brainstorming exercises you'll ever use for generating ideas for your report. I call it "*alphabetizing*".

Starting with the letter "A" in the alphabet, literally begin thinking of events, places, people, items, verbs, ideas, etc. that begin with that letter and are related to the topic of your report. The goal is to go all the way to "Z". This is a great way to brainstorm ideas.

Example: If you are writing a product related to traveling to Orlando, you might have...

A = Airports
B = Business travel
C = Choosing hotels
D = Dining
E = Epcot
F = Free tickets
G = Golfing

After you've gotten keywords for each of the 26 letters of the alphabet, jot down any notes about each of those entries that you want to mention in your report. And just like that you've got 26 ideas to write about in your report. If you just wrote 1/4 page on each of them, you'd

```
have almost 7 pages of content!
------------------------
    .
```

Note: In my Content Writing Made Easy package I share with you dozens of "idea starters" to help you brainstorm a virtually unlimited set of topics. **Plus you'll also get fill-in-the-blank templates to help you create your short report and any other content you need to write. Check it out: <u>www.contentwritingmadeeasy.com</u>.**

So, that's how you "*plan out your report by brainstorming ideas*". That's the "P" of the "P.A.G.E.S." system. Now, let's move on to step 2 which is...

Step #2: <u>A</u>RRANGE your ideas sequentially or systematically.

This step doesn't require a lot of explanation, but let me go ahead and just touch on this a bit for clarification purposes.

There are <u>two basic ways</u> to "arrange" your ideas once you have them all jotted down - in other words "organize" them so they make sense. These two ways are "sequentially" and "systematically".

Sequentially:

> That is, you would organize your ideas in chronological steps. In any kind of "how-to" information there is a logical order in which steps occur. You would simply outline your report based on what comes first and then what

comes after that. Step 1 is... Step 2 is... Step 3 is...

Now, as a rule of thumb, I recommend that you keep the total number of steps to something in SINGLE DIGITS. No more than 9 steps. Anything more than that could be viewed as "too much work" in the eyes of your readers. So, organize all of your ideas in 9 or less steps, beginning with the step that comes first and ending with the step that comes last.

Systematically:

The other option is to organize things "systematically". In other words, you'd group ideas together based on their logical relationship to each other.

Example 1: If your title is "*5 Keys to Saving Your Marriage Now*", then that's the basic framework for your outline. You divide things into sections or parts, whatever you want to call them, one for each of the 5 keys. Key #1 is a section. Key #2 is a section. Key #3 is a section. And so forth. All of your ideas would fall into one of your 5 keys.

Example 2: If you have a LOT of different ideas, such as "*101 Homeschooling Tips for First-Time Parents*", then find 5-9 main topics to group them into. For example, "tips for finding the right curriculum", "tips for planning field trips," "tips for creating a learning environment," "tips for social interaction" and so forth.

Note: Now, let me give you a recommendation on arranging ideas that I've found to be very important over the years.

While you want ALL of your report to be quality content that's useful to your customer, let's face it, some points are stronger than others. There are some things you'll be sharing that are just better or more important or less known than others. It's important that you fire these FIRST and LAST.

That is, you want your best work (if possible, understandably "steps" come in whatever order they appear) to be in the first few pages and then finish strong in the last few pages. If you have any content that's "weaker" than the rest, then you'll want to include it somewhere in the middle if it's important enough to share at all. It's not that you're trying to "hide" anything, it's simply that you want to minimize your weaknesses and showcase your strengths.

That same rule of thumb can be used with any "sub-ideas" you have for each of your main points (your "ways" or "steps", etc.): your strongest sub-ideas come first and last with the others mixed in the middle somewhere.

And with that, we're on to step 3...

Step #3: GROW your content by "filling in the blanks".

By this point you should have a nice outline created from all of your ideas. Now, it's simply a matter of "filling in the blanks". That is, write a few paragraphs of meaty information for each of your points listed in your outline. That's all it takes. (You should have at least 26 "points" listed from the alphabetizing exercise.) Remember, this is only 7-15 pages that you're striving for.

What I do is just a little bit of math. I take the total number of pages that I want and divide it by the total number of ideas that I've written down so I can see how much I need to write for each point.

> Example: Let's suppose I want to create a 10 page report on my topic. Let's further suppose that I have 20 "ideas" that I've brainstormed to share in the report that I've arranged in 5 different sections. Doing the math, we find that I need 1/2 page of content per idea in order to meet the page requirement. So, I begin writing the first point and when I've reached 1/2 page, I know I can quit anytime I finalize the thought I'm sharing.

Some of your points will require less space to share than the numbers would demand. That's okay, because some of your points will go over. It all balances out in the end, and it's not an exact science. It's just a way to keep things balanced.

It really doesn't even matter that you do the math ... as long as you do the writing. Simply write a few paragraphs explanation for each of the points. Don't be afraid to mix in some humor. Inject your own personality into the writing.

Now, what I want to do for you before we move on to the next steps is to share some "content templates" with you now that will also help you with the writing part of content creation.

Basically, here's how it works. I'm going to provide you with 20 content templates. Each one consists of an opening sentence that you can apply to any portion of your product where you might need some additional ideas for content.

Content Template #1:

If I could sum up _____ in _____ steps, here is what they would be _____ "

Where you see the "blanks" you just complete the blanks with whatever topic you are going to be discussing in that section of your product.

> Example: "If I could sum up doing business online in 3 steps, here is what they would be..."
>
> I might choose...
>
> Step 1: Develop a product.
> Step 2: Build a website.
> Step 3: Promote.

So, you begin a section by opening with the above provided sentence by completing the blank sections with whatever topic you plan on discussing in that section.

Some other examples might include...

> "If I could sum up **creating an ezine article** in **5** steps,
> here is what they would be..."

> "If I could sum up **losing weight and getting in shape** in **4** steps,
> here is what they would be..."

> "If I could sum up **learning to play guitar** in **3** steps,
> here is what they would be..."

> "If I could sum up **restoring antique vehicles** in **5** steps,
> here is what they would be..."

Your opening sentence sets the stage for that section. Just insert your own topic in the template and you're ready to begin. Next, you write supporting paragraphs for each of the three steps, which can be as little as one paragraph, but should be preferably 3-4 paragraphs per step.

Content Template #2:

"One of the things that the majority of folks find most challenging about _____ is _____..."

> Example: "One of the things that the majority of folks find most challenging about ***selling online*** is to ***generate website traffic***."

Some other examples might include...

> "One of the things that the majority of folks find most challenging
> about **losing weight** is to **stay motivated**."

> "One of the things that the majority of folks find most challenging
> about **playing guitar** is to **memorize where their fingers go for each chord**."

> "One of the things that the majority of folks find most challenging
> about **the game of golf** is to **hit a good chip shot**."

> "One of the things that the majority of folks find most challenging
> about **buying a new car** is to **make certain they get the best price**."

That section of your report is then super easy to write.

First, I'd briefly describe the challenge itself. Why is it so difficult? What problems do most folks face when attempting to do it? What makes it challenging? Spend 2-3 paragraphs describing the challenge itself. Then, suggest a solution. Yep, you've got the answers. And you're willing to share them. So, offer some advice on how to overcome the challenge. Outline 4 or 5 tips for solving the problem. Each tip only needs to be 1 paragraph in length, but it all adds up to a great deal of content.

Content Template #3:

"A little known secret about _____ is
_____"

Some variations on this theme include...

A seldom used tactic
An often misunderstood
An often overlooked
The best kept secret
One of the most powerful

Examples would be...

> *"A little known secret about **buying a new car** is to **understand the sticker price.**"*

> *"A little known secret about **hiring a ghostwriter** is to **NEVER accept the lowest bid.**"*

> *"A little known secret about **losing weight fast** is to **eat smaller meals throughout the day**"*

> *"A little known secret about **creating a budget** is to **allot money for entertainment**"*

Content Template #4:

"Perhaps one of the biggest reasons that people fail in _____ is _____"

Examples would be:

"Perhaps one of the biggest reasons that people fail
*in **business online** is **a lack of training**."*

"Perhaps one of the biggest reasons that people fail
*in **creating content** is **they don't buy ContentWritingMadeEasy.com!** ☺ ."*

"Perhaps one of the biggest reasons that people fail
*in **losing weight** is **a lack of discipline**."*

"Perhaps one of the biggest reasons that people fail
*in **house breaking poodles** is **the wrong approach**."*

After exposing what is perhaps the biggest reason that people fail in achieving their desired outcome, give the reader several quick tips on how to avoid failure, specifically mentioning how to achieve success.

See how easy this is when you just have a starting point?

You could probably easily work in 4 or 5 tips about achieving success in a particular area. You could probably weave in a short 3-5 step system for achieving success in a particular area. You could probably pose and answer several questions relating to success in a particular area.

It's all about having something to begin with, which is the purpose of our content templates here.

Content Template #5:

*"The one thing I always get asked about
_____ is _____."*

Examples would be:

> *"The one thing I always get asked about **dieting**
> is **can I lose weight fast**?"*

> *"The one thing I always get asked about
> **homeschooling**
> is **will it hurt my child's social skills**?"*

> *"The one thing I always get asked about **online
> dating**
> is **it safe**?"*

> *"The one thing I always get asked about
> **relieving headaches**
> is **what can I do to avoid them altogether**?"*

Fire away your most asked question and then answer
it. Provide them with as many tips or steps in your
answer as you can.

Content Template #6:

*"The number one mistake that beginning _____
make is that
they _____."*

Examples:

> *"The number on mistake that beginning
> **marketers** make is that*

*they **don't set up a sales funnel.***"

*"The number one mistake that **beginning bodybuilders** make is that*
*they **go crazy buying supplements, but they don't pay close attention to the rest of their diet.***"

*"The number one mistake that beginning **copywriters** make is that*
*they **don't create a swipe file or template set like the one available at ContentWritingMadeEasy.com**.*"

Once again, this sort of statement just opens the door for you to talk about how to avoid a mistake like this. Depending on the mistake, you might offer a step-by-step approach for avoiding the mistake, or your might offer a series of tips and tricks.

Content Template #7:

"You've probably heard people telling you _____. However, what may surprise you is that _____. Let me explain..."

Examples:

*"You've probably heard people telling you **that you need to exercise to lose weight**. However, what may surprise you is that **that you can lose 10 pounds without ever setting foot in a gym**. Let me explain..."*

> *"You've probably heard people telling you **you'll need to spend a good year or two learning how to write copy**. However, what may surprise you is that you can get started today by using a system like ContentWritingMadeEasy.com**. Let me explain..."***

> *"You've probably heard people telling you **yams won't grow in your cool climate with the short growing season.** However, what may surprise you is that you can **quickly and easily build a greenhouse that lets you get a jump on the growing season**. Let me explain..."*

The idea here is to take some commonly held notion about getting some benefit, and letting people know they can still get that benefit even if they don't have some particular prerequisite.

In other words, give them an alternative. This works well for people who don't like the traditional methods or are unable to follow the traditional methods for achieving some result.

Content Template #8:

"There's one little trick the experts do that virtually no one else does – and it makes the difference between _____ and/versus _____."

Examples:

> *"There's one little trick the experts do that virtually no one else does – and it makes the difference between **struggling to find your***

abs *and* ***winning bodybuilding competitions.***"

"*There's one little trick the experts do that virtually no one else does – and it makes the difference between* ***having a garden overrun with pests*** *versus* ***growing lush, delicious vegetables in a pest-free garden****.*"

"*There's one little trick the experts do that virtually no one else does – and it makes the difference between* ***humiliating yourself on the golf course*** *versus* ***making your golfing buddies jealous with your impressive drives****.*"

In the above template I used the word "trick," but you can certainly use a similar word such as "secret."

The reason this content opener is so powerful is because it arouses curiosity – people need to read on just to see what the trick is that separates the pros from those getting mediocre results.

Naturally, the next few paragraphs or pages will reveal that trick to readers.

Content Template #9:

"*Most people who're looking to _____ want to save time and money. One of the best ways to do that is to _____.*"

Examples:

> *"Most people who're looking to **buy their first home** want to save time and money. One of the best ways to do that is to **get your credit in order before you start shopping around**."*

> *"Most people who're looking to start a **content-marketing business** want to save time and money.*

> *"Most people who're looking to **get quality health care** also want to save time and money. One of the best ways to do that is to **compare health care providers carefully**."*

For this template I used "saving time and money" as the thing people want, simply because these are somewhat universal desires.

However, you can replace "time and money" with some factor that is important to your readers.

Then the next several paragraphs or pages would details the steps readers need to take to get this benefit.

Content Template #10:

"If there's one thing that I wished I had done differently when I first started _____, it would be / I would have _____."

Examples:

> *"If there's one thing that I wished I had done differently when I first started **dieting**, it would be to **not slash my calories so drastically in***

the beginning."

*"If there's one thing that I wished I had done differently when I first started **my own business**, I would have **set up a sales funnel right away**."*

*"If there's one thing that I wished I had done differently when I first started **training for a marathon**, I would have **invested more money in really good pair of running shoes.**"*

Here's another opportunity to talk about mistakes, except this time you add a personal touch by telling your own stories about mistakes you made. After this opener, you can go on to talk about how to avoid this mistake – and what to do instead.

Content Template #11:

"If you look around, it seems like most people who _____ have _____. The good news is that _____."

Examples:

*"If you look around, it seems like most people **who land the best jobs** have **advanced college degrees**. The good news is that **you too can land your dream job – even if you don't have a Master's degree."***

*"If you look around, it seems like most people who have **high-response sales letters** have **on-staff, highly paid copywriters to create**

*these letters. The good news is that **you too can start creating high-converting sales materials using ContentWritingMadeEasy.com.***"

*"If you look around, it seems like most people who have **washboard abs** also have **plenty of free time to get to the gym and eat right**. The good news is that **you too can get your six-pack – even if you have just 15 minutes a day.**"*

This is another instance where you can talk about some factor that most people think they need to have in order to succeed, such as an advanced degree to get a good job. Then your content can go on to tell people how to get the results they want even if they don't possess this particular factor.

Content Template #12:

"Research studies suggest _____. But is it true?"

Examples:

*"Research studies suggest **that eating healthy fats like peanuts and fish oil can help you lose weight more quickly**. But is it true?"*

*"Research studies suggest **that lonely people are more likely to die prematurely.** But is it true?"*

*"Research studies suggest **that poodles and***

border collies are among the smartest dogs on the planet. *But is it true?"*

In this case, you use this content opener to arouse curiosity. After this opener, you then go on to detail:

1. What the research study is all about.

2. How this study impacts members of your target market.

3. Steps and tips your readers can use to make the most of this information.

Content Template #13:

"Let me share with you a story about how [I or someone else]
went from _____ to _____."

Examples:

*"Let me share with you a story about how I went from **couch potato to long-distance runner in just a few short months**."*

*"Let me share with you a story about how John went **from truck driver to six-figure content marketer in less than one year**."*

*"Let me share with you a story about how Susan went from **100 pounds overweight to swimsuit model in about a year**."*

This content opener gives you the opportunity to share a story, which is a good way to engage readers and connect with them on an emotional level.

You can use this opener to inspire and motivate your readers. After you've shared the story, be sure to detail steps and tips for how your readers can get their own good results.

Content Template #14:

"If you're like most people, you're looking for a way to skip the learning curve
and start _____. Here are three tips for
_____..."

Examples:

> *"If you're like most people, you're looking for a way to skip the learning curve and **start turning back the hands of time quickly.** Here are three tips for **getting rid of those wrinkles and fine lines**..."*

> *"If you're like most people, you're looking for a way to skip the learning curve and start **building your profitable business as soon as possible**. Here are three tips for **getting your business off the ground fast**..."*

> *"If you're like most people, you're looking for a way to skip the learning curve and start **enjoying lower scores on the golf course**. Here are three tips for **shaving strokes off your game**..."*

No matter what type of results your readers are seeking, chances are they want these results as quickly and as effortlessly as possible.

This opener sets you up to talk about three tips (or more) that will help readers get the results they want, fast.

Content Template #15:

"Some people say _____. But the truth is, _____."

Examples:

> *"Some people say **cardio is the best exercise for fat loss**. But the truth is, **the wrong kind of cardio can make you skinny fat**."*

> *"Some people say **affiliate marketing is the best type of content marketing business**. But the truth is, **creating your own products is more likely to bring you bigger profits**."*

> *"Some people say organic pest control is ineffective and time consuming. But the truth is, **those folks just haven't learned the latest secrets of organic gardening**."*

No matter what topic you're covering in your short report, it's likely that the market in general offers conflicting information. Some experts say one thing, while other experts say another.

You can use this content opener to share your opinion on which method is best, or you can even use it to shatter commonly held myths. After this opener, you can then go on to detail why the commonly held notions are wrong, as well as list steps for a better way to get results.

Content Template #16:

*"Do you think you need _____ to _____?
Then you're in for some good news."*

Examples:

> *"Do you think you need **a college degree to get a high-paying job**? Then you're in for some good news."*
>
> *"Do you think you need a **lot of money to start your own home business**? Then you're in for some good news."*
>
> *"Do you think you need personal training or some high-priced diet food to lose weight? Then you're in for some good news."*

This is another content template that arouses curiosity, as well as sets you up to talk about why people don't need some prerequisite in order to get the results they want. While you can certainly use this template at any point within your short report, it makes a great opening line if your report teaches a method that doesn't rely on people possessing some skill, experience, or material possession.

Content Template #17:

"Recently, the news reports _____. And you might be wondering
how this will impact _____."

Examples:

> *"Recently, the news reports **have suggested that the Whiz Bang Drug is going to be banned in the United States**. And you might be wondering how this will impact **your diabetes treatment**."*

> *"Recently, the news reports have suggested **that the economy is about to collapse again**. And you might be wondering how this will impact **your retirement**."*

> *"Recently, the news reports have suggested that **student loan rates are going to rise alongside tuition rates.** And you might be wondering how this will impact **your children's futures – will they end up living with you when they're 30?**"*

If you're working in an evergreen niche and creating evergreen content, then you have to be a little careful about using this particular template, as it can easily "date" your content (which means in short order your content can be outdated). As such, only use this template if you intend to regularly update your short report.

Content Template #18:

"_____ might seem like a risky way to _____, but/which is why _____."

Examples:

> **"Extreme low-calorie diets** might seem like a risky way to lose weight, but **new evidence suggests a zig-zag method can produce safe, effective results**."
>
> **"Investing in the stock market** might seem like a risky way to fund your retirement, which is why **so many people are turning to this brilliantly simple investment strategy**."
>
> **"Using creatine** might seem like a risky way for teenagers to help recover from athletic activities, but **experts are now saying that it's not as dangerous as the media makes it out to be**."

This is a good template to use if the information you're sharing might be a bit controversial.

You can take <u>two approaches</u> with this template:

> 1. Agree that some method is indeed risky, and then go on to detail a less-risky yet very effective alternative method.
>
> 2. Show readers why the method isn't as risky as they thought. Your report can even detail tips and steps for reducing risk using this particular method.

Content Template #19:

"Imagine this: _____."

Examples:

*"Imagine this: **you are 50 pounds heavier and feel younger than ever**.*

*"Imagine this: **you just published your first book and it hits the New York Times bestseller list."***

*"Imagine this: **you can quit your job because your new business is pulling six figures a year.***"

This content template gets your readers to imagine themselves receiving great results. The first line describes what the result is. The rest of the paragraph can go on to elaborate on the benefits of getting this result.

You can then spend the next several pages describing how, exactly, the readers can achieve these results for themselves.

Content Template #20:

"Quick, what's the first thing that springs to mind when you think of _____? If you're like most people, you answered _____. But here's something that may surprise you: _____."

Examples:

*"Quick, what's the first thing that springs to mind when you think of **dieting**? If you're like most people, you answered **hunger pangs**. But here's something that may surprise you: **you***

don't need to starve yourself to lose weight."

*"Quick, what's the first thing that springs to mind when you think of **bodybuilding**? If you're like most people, you answered **steroids**. But here's something that may surprise you: **you can get a muscular beach body without taking a single supplement**."*

*"Quick, what's the first thing that springs to mind when you think of **training for a marathon**? If you're like most people, you answered shin **splints and side aches**. But here's something that may surprise you: **you too can train for a marathon without feeling all those aches and pains.***

This content template is a good introduction to talking about some factor that your readers tend to find unpleasant, such as the above examples of hunger pangs, steroids and pain.

Your next several pages can then detail how readers can avoid these unpleasant "side effects" that are commonly associated with the process you're describing.

So, those are the twenty content templates. Plug in your responses and you're off and running. Now, let's move on to step number 4...

Step #4: EXTRACT bullet points for your ad copy while you write. In an upcoming section, I'm going to share with you how to write a "mini-sales letter" to convince your list members to buy your special report.

What is going to be invaluable to you in that part of the process is what you do right here in step four of your content creation.

With any good sales letter, there will be a "bullet list" of benefit statements.

You've seen them at sales letters online. They offer encapsulated glimpses into what the product or service being offered means to you in terms of its benefit to you.

What I like to do is develop these bullet points as I'm writing the content. Over and over again, I've found myself with things in my reports like, "the fastest way I know to..." or "3 of the easiest ways to..." or "my own secret weapon for..." or "if you don't do anything else, make sure you do this..."

So, when I find myself inserting those things, I stop at the completion of my thought process and I write down a variation of the statement that I made for use as a bullet point.

Some examples include:

- The hands down, fastest way to double your affiliate commission checks!

- 3 of the easiest ways to turn private label content in your own multiple streams of profit empire in about 30 minutes per week!

- Revealed: my own secret weapon for getting completely free search engine traffic without any tricks or gimmicks!

```
(Hint: You can download it from a
freeware site and virtually NO ONE knows
you can use it this way!)
```

- ```
  Warning: If you don't do anything else
  with your blog, make sure you do this one
  "trick" for getting bigger Adsense®
  commissions. (Unless, of course, you just
  don't like extra money with no extra
  work!)
  ```

Notice, of course, that they are in bullet form. ☺

You'll undoubtedly notice that you make similar statements throughout writing the content for your special report. Take just a few seconds to extract those statements so you can use them on your sales letter as bulleted benefits. I recommend that you grab about 10-12 of them for the sales page for these kinds of special reports.

And then, it's off to the final step...

Step #5: <u>S</u>MOOTH out the rough spots to complete the report. Once you've written the content for your special report, you'll want to fine-tune it. Generally speaking, there are three things that I recommend you do in putting on the finishing touches for your report...

- **<u>PAD</u>.** That is, look for areas of your report that need further explanation. Are there any areas that are not clearly explained? Are there areas that are noticeably weaker than others? Make sure your points are understandable. Try to add in as many examples as possible to better illustrate the points. Toss in a few more tips
  ```

here and there where needed. You can add interview transcripts, quotes, research and other bits of information to get the points across better and add a bit more meat to the report.

- **<u>POLISH</u>.** Use different fonts to distinguish areas of your content. Change colors. Use alternative styles such as bold face, italics and underline. Indent text where appropriate. Use bullet points. (Especially on lists.)Insert headers, footers and graphics (just don't overdo it!) Make your special report look, well, special! ☺ (We'll talk more about this in our next section.)

- **<u>PROOFREAD</u>.** The final "smoothing out" you need to make certain you do is to proofread your entire document for typographic and grammatical errors. Better still would be to allow someone else who is qualified to do it for you. While this isn't a deal breaker by any means (quality of content is MUCH more important than quality of grammar in information based reports), it certainly is a good idea to put your best foot forward.

So, there you have it, the "P.A.G.E.S." system. Each letter (P - A - G - E - S) stands for one of the five steps in the system...

```
P - PLAN out your report by brainstorming
ideas.
A - ARRANGE your ideas sequentially or
systematically.
G - GROW your content by "filling in the
blanks".
E - EXTRACT bullet points for your ad
copy while you write.
```

```
S - SMOOTH out the rough spots to
complete the report.
```

Well, that's a wrap for this section.

Let's move on to our next section...

How To Package, Price And Position
Your Small Report For Mega-Success

Now that you've written the actual content for your small report, you'll want to get it ready to sell by putting on a few finishing touches.

So, let's spend some time talking about some ancillary things you need to focus on – primarily *"packaging"*, *"pricing"* and *"positioning"*.

First up, let's look at "packaging"...

Part 1: <u>PACKAGING</u>. When it comes to *"packaging"* your small report, there are two basic things you want to address: the *"contents"* and the *"cosmetics"*.

Contents:

In addition to the information of your small report, there are other *"pages"* that are needed in order to complete its construction. In order of appearance within your finished report, they are...

(1) **Title page**. This typically will include the title of your report, any subtitle, your name as author and possibly your website address, contact information and any graphics you might want to include.

(2) **Legal page**. This necessary page of your special report would include copyright information, disclaimers, terms of usage and any extra special disclosures or instructions you might have. There's an example "legal page" included in our forms bonus with this package that you can refer to in creating your own.

(3) **Author page**. You should always include a page about yourself in your special report for a couple of solid reasons: it allows your readers to identify with you, thus establishing a "trust" relationship; it allows you to inform the reader of other resources you may offer such as your newsletter, other reports and products, web site, etc.

(4) **Special Offer page**. One of the biggest mistakes you can make in creating a special report is NOT including a "special offer" page. I always make certain I devote a separate page – up front after my author page – to making some kind of special offer to the reader. Three of my favorite ways to use this "special offer" page are...

- <u>DISCOUNT</u> on a related offer.

   That is, I would mention a product or service or additional special report, directly related to the material in the report the reader is currently viewing. Specifically, I would offer a **one-time discount** for this additional purchase since they had already made a purchase.

- <u>DEAL</u> for a related offer.

   That is, I would mention some **free incentive** that I'll give them as an extra bonus should they purchase an additional featured product or service related to the content of the report they are viewing. This broadens my possibilities in that I can not only mention an offer of my own, but can also promote an affiliate program if I want to do so.

- <u>DEADLINE</u> for a related offer.

   That is, I would mention a product or service that has a deadline or some kind of limit imposed upon it to create a sense of urgency for the reader to buy. Again, this additional "special offer" would be related to information contained in the report the reader is currently viewing. This time, the additional offer would be available "only for the first 25 who buy" or "only for 72 hours after your original purchase date" or some other similar restriction.

(5)   Table of contents. (Optional) This is the one page of your small report that is optional. Typically, if you have a short report, let's say 7 pages, you wouldn't really need a table of contents. Only use a table of contents if your report is 25-30 pages and has distinct chapter separations that are worth noting in advance.

(6)   Report. Next comes the report itself. As we've talked about previously, this would be, on average, 7-15 pages in length, with a maximum of 30 pages. After your featured information, there is one final element to the "contents" of your small report...

(7)   Backend page. There should always be some kind of "backend" offer at the conclusion of your special report. This can be something as blatant as a full-blown advertisement for a high-ticket product or something as subtle as a brief listing of your other special reports available for purchase. These products could include reports, ebooks, membership sites, videos, physical products, services, coaching, workshops, and similar items.

Your <u>Minimum</u> Backend: "Recommended Resources"

What I consider to be a minimum is a list of about 3-4 *"recommend resources"* that are related to the content of your special report. These can either be your own related offers or those you promote as an

---

affiliate.

> Example: If your special report consists
> of "Ten Keys To Homeschooling Success",
> you might list these (made up) additional
> "recommended resources" at the conclusion
> of your report...
>
> - Time Management for Homeschoolers
> - The Beginner's Guide to
>   Homeschooling
> - 101 Ready-Made Lesson Plans for
>   Homeschoolers

Hint: Look for recommended resources that have a "freebie" available at their main sales page, such as a free report, newsletter or tutorials. This will allow you to add more value to your own report, provide a service to your customer, generate more interest and response, and ultimately get more readers to the additional sales pages where you earn commissions on purchases made.

Regardless of whether you choose to include a subtle list of resources or a direct advertisement for a product, the key to success is to make sure the offer is tightly related to your short report. Indeed, your short report can't possibly cover every aspect of some problem, so your backend offer should be the next logical step for your readers.

> Example: let me give you an example.
> Let's suppose your short report teaches
> people how to eat right to lose weight.

Your backend offer might be one of the following:

- An advanced dieting product which includes exercise tips, an advanced nutrition program and advice about diet aids and supplements.
- Membership for a weight-loss support site.
- Subscription to a meal-planning site.
- Another short report that covers another aspect of weight loss, such as strength training and/or cardio exercise.
- A physical product to help them lose weight, such as prepackaged food, vitamins or other diet supplements, or exercise equipment.

Again, the idea is that your backend offer should give your readers another step or solution to their overall problem.

Now, you might be tempted to recommend a whole bunch of related resources that your readers can use to solve their problems. However, if you give your readers too many options, they'll feel overwhelmed... and it's less likely that they'll click on any of them.

What's more, if the back of your 7-15 page report is full of several pages of advertisements, your reader is going to feel "ripped off." They're going to feel like they paid good money in order to read a promotion. It doesn't even matter if your short report solved their problems and gave them good advice. It's their perception that matters. If they see several pages of ads, they may feel a bit "cheated."

So, what you need to do is pick out from one to four good products to advertise in the back of your report. In order to make this strategy as effective as possible, follow these tips:

- **Tell your readers why this resource is valuable to them**. Don't just list the name of the resource and assume that your readers will click on it and/or understand why they should give it. Instead, take them by the hand and specifically tell them three or four of the top benefits of this particular product.

  Example: "Now that you just learned how to use content to effortlessly grow your business, your next step is to start creating this content. Problem is, writing a lot of content takes a lot of work— seems like you spend more time staring at a blank screen. And hiring a ghostwriter to create it for you is extremely expensive.

  The good news is that now you too can create content quickly and easily using the ContentWritingMadeEasy.com package. This package includes dozens upon dozens of "plug and play" templates, examples and tips to help you create content faster and easier than ever. You'll get templates for blog posts, articles, emails, sales letters and much more.

No matter what kind of content you need to create, www.contentwritingmadeeasy.com is your quick and easy solution for generating high-quality content on a budget."

- **Give them a clear call to action with a reason to buy now.** After you list the benefits of the offer, you need to specifically tell your readers what you'd like them to do (click on the link and buy the product) – and give them a good reason to do it now.

Example: "Listen, if you need to create content, then you need ContentWritingMadeEasy.com. There's no better way to create content quickly and easily. Never again will writer's block or poor writing skills keep you from creating the content you need. Check it out for yourself right now by going to www.contentwritingmadeeasy.com – and do it now while you can still get it at a great price!

One last tip before I leave the topic of backend products...

Ideally what you want to do is to choose offers that not only help your prospects the most, but also those that put the most money in your pocket. To that end, you may want to do some testing to see which offers your prospects respond to the best.

If you have a mailing list, one way to do this is to "split test" your offers, meaning you randomly divide your list into at least two groups, and then promote a different product to each of these groups. This will give you an idea of which product gives you the best response rate—and then you can promote this offer at the end of your short report.

Another way to do it is to test with the report itself. You can do this by creating two versions of the report, one which promotes "Product A" and the other promotes "Product B" on the last page. Half of your short-report customers will get the first version and the other half of your customers will get the second version of this report. You can then use a tracking tool (like Google Analytics) to see which links get the most clicks and which product puts the most profit in your product. Once you've determined this, then you can have all your customers download the version of the report that creates the most profits for you.

So, those are the chief things you'll want to include in packaging your special report as far as the "contents" are concerned. What about the "cosmetics"? Let's talk about that for a few minutes...

Cosmetics:

We've talked about WHAT to include in your special report. Now, let's turn our attention to HOW you should include those things. In other words, how do these materials LOOK? Appearance is important. Very important.

There's a big difference between something scribbled in crayons and something etched in calligraphy. While we aren't striving for a work of art here, it is our aim to create something aesthetically pleasing rather than something that proves to be an eyesore.

So, let me briefly mention 8 things you'll want to do in order to sharpen the appearance of your special report as you finish up "packaging" the materials...

(1) **Header and Footer**. The layout of your content pages begins with a "header and footer". These appear on every page of your special report, with the exception of your title page (page one). Not surprisingly, the "header" appears at the very top of the page and the "footer" appears at the bottom of the page.

Example Header: If you look to the top of the page you are now reading, you'll see an example "header". I most often use the title of the work in boldface style, with a horizontal line beneath it to separate it from the remainder of the page.

Example Footer: By turning your attention to the bottom of the page, you'll see an example "footer". Note the use of copyright information to the left, my website address to the right and the page number in the middle. Additionally, there is a horizontal line above the text to separate it from the remainder of the page.

(2) **Margins.** I have observed some marked differences in the size of margins in the many years I've been reading information products. Some blatantly use 1.5"-2.0" margins in an attempt to produce "more pages" with the same amount of text. These same folks use 20 point text for the same purpose. Resist the temptation to join them. You don't need to attempt any sleight of hand tactics – which are quite obvious, by the way – to "pad" your length. It's not quantity we're after in special reports, it's quality. The point is to be to the point! I recommend .75" margins with additional space at the top and bottom for your header and footer.

(3) **Fonts.** There are a lot of well-used fonts that you can choose from in creating your special report. Some of the more prevalent are Times New Roman, Helvetica, Arial, Courier, Tahoma and Verdana. To be completely honest, I don't have a preferred font that I use. Any of these I've mentioned work well. What I don't recommend is trying to get cute by using some of the fancier fonts you'll find in your word processor. While it may look nice at first, many other fonts become difficult to read after a period of time and could detract from your work.

```
Note:  One thing I DO recommend is
that you use THREE different fonts in
·your special report.  One for
boldface, larger headlines. (Such as
Tahoma).  Another for the main bulk of
your content. (Such as Verdana) And a
third one for isolating special text
to make it stand out. (Such as
Courier)  You'll note that I do this
repeatedly throughout my reports.  In
fact, what you're reading now is in
Courier New in order to bring
attention to it.
--------------------------
```

It's also a good idea to stick with standard 12 point text size. In the words of Goldilocks, "*this one's just right*".

(4)   Headlines. When you arrive at new chapters, distinctions, listings or any other kind of "separation / divider" in your special report, re-focus your readers attention by using boldface, larger text headlines. I generally use 18 point Tahoma in bold style. This serves a dual purpose: firstly, to separate key sections and thoughts from the remainder of the text; secondly, to add another design element to the appearance of the text. While I wouldn't consider myself a master of any design aspects (I'm a writer and marketer, not a graphic designer!) I have been told repeatedly over the years how attractive my materials are. So, feel free to take a look at the presentation of headlines in this report to get an idea of how to use them in your own.

(5) **Indentions and Boxes**. Indentions and boxes are two more nice "cosmetics" you can use to improve the flow of reading and add another dimension to your report's layout. I recommend that you use indentions and boxes to separate key thoughts, create bullet lists, define words and expressions, provide case studies, give a closer look, make a recommendation, offer an example and any other way you may want to provide additional details.

(6) **Styles**. One of the most commonly used design elements of your special report should be font "styles" such as *italics*, **bold** and underline. These are especially useful in creating distinctions and placing emphasis on important points or inflections. Please note that the **numbering** and **type of cosmetic** in this list of packaging ideas is highlighted in a font style. And, please further note that I just drew your attention to the words "numbering", "and" and "type of cosmetic" in the previous sentence by using font styles. Very effective in streamlining your content and getting your point across in important spots.

(7) **Colors | Highlights**. While I don't change colors of the fonts I use very often, there are times when using an additional color such as red or **blue** can be useful – especially if you're wanting to **draw special attention** to a point you're making. Another option is to

highlight your text in order to make it significantly stand out. If you're going to highlight, I'd recommend that you use a yellow background with a boldface text.

(8) **Graphics | Screenshots | Photographs**. Finally, I want to mention that there will be times when you'll want to use graphics, screenshots and photographs in your special report. I have a simple rule of thumb when it comes to these two special agents of design: use them when they are helpful or needed.

- If you're writing a tutorial for using a software program, then screenshots of the application's interface would be helpful, thus making them a good idea.

- If you're writing a report on weight loss and want to include "before and after" photographs to prove your results and / or motivate the reader, then that's a suitable use.

- If you're wanting to insert some animated graphic of a clock because you happened to mention a clock in the paragraph, that's not necessarily the best use of your space.

One Final Note: Before we move on to "pricing" your special report, there's one final thing I need to address about "packaging". People used to create "ebooks" in a variety of forms. However, today the gold standard is to use the PDF format. Not only is it easy for you to create your downloadable file, but people using both Windows-based and Mac computers can read your report. In other words, it's cross-platform friendly.

Now, I personally used Adobe Acrobat Professional to create my PDFs in the click of one button. However, it can be a bit pricey. That's why I'm going to offer two alternatives to you:

- Use a free PDF tool like PDF Architect alongside your regular word processing software.

- Use a free word processing suite like Open Office.

Let's take a quick look at how these options work...

Tutorial: Using PDF Architect to Create Your Report

If you'd like to use your own word processing software (like Microsoft Word) to create you report, then you'll need a method to convert the .doc or .docx document into a .pdf. That's where PDF Architect comes in.

Here's how to do it:

1. Download and install PDF Architect

Go to http://www.pdfarchitect.org/ to download the latest version of PDF Architect. Save it to your computer, and then double click the file to start the installation process. Follow the prompts to complete the installation process.

What this software does is installs itself into Microsoft Word as if it was a printer. So in order to convert a file to .pdf, you go through the initial steps as if you were going to print the file, but you choose the "Print to PDF Option" rather than choosing to print to your hardware. Read on for the specifics...

2. Open Microsoft Word. Or open a similar word processing program.

3. Open your report file in Microsoft Word.

This is your working document where you've been creating your report. This is a .doc or .docx file, usually, unless you've saved it in a different format.

Click on the Windows logo (or "File" menu, in some systems) in the upper right side of the screen, choose "open" and then navigate to your report file.

4. Convert your .doc or .docx to a PDF.

The way you do this is pretend like you're going to print your report. So click on the Windows logo (or "File" menu, in some systems) in the upper left hand side of your Microsoft Word screen, scroll down to "Print," and then choose the "Print as PDF Option" as shown here:

4. Convert your .doc or .docx to a PDF.

The way you do this is pretend like you're going to print your report. So click on the Windows logo icon in the upper left hand side of your Microsoft Word screen, scroll down to "Print," and then choose the "Print as PDF Option" as shown here:

It will ask you to choose your file name – so choose a descriptive name that makes sense (e.g., "dog-training-report"). PDF Architect will automatically add the ".pdf" extension to the end of the report. Be sure to take note of where on your hard drive you're saving the .pdf document.

Once you start the conversion, PDF Architect will keep you informed of what it is doing (e.g., "conversion started" and "conversion finished").

Step 5: Check the resulting file.

Once the PDF has finished converting, PDF Architect will open up your PDF so that you can review your report.

Be sure to scroll through and make sure everything looks right. If not, go back and edit your Word document and convert it again.

If it looks the way you want it to look, congrats – you're done! Now you just need to upload this file to your website so that your customers can access it. (Instructions for uploading files are included elsewhere in this guide.

That's one quick and easy way to create a PDF report. Here's another...

Tutorial: Using Open Office to Create Your PDF Report

If you are open to using a slightly different word processor, then I suggest you use the free Open Office word processing suite, which includes a PDF converter and works on both Windows and Mac platforms.

Here's how to do it...

Step 1: Download and install Open Office.

You'll need to go to www.openoffice.org to get the download file—be sure to note where on your computer you save the installation file. Then double click on this file on your hard drive to begin the installation process.

Step 2: Start or open your file using Open Office.

Double click on the software, register it if you haven't already done so, and then choose "Text Document."

At this point, you can either:

- Open up an existing text document that you created using a different word processor.

- Create your report from scratch using Open Office, which is user-friendly and very similar to other word processors you've used.

Be sure to save the file.

Step 3: Export to PDF.

Now it's time to convert your text document to PDF. All you have to do is click on "File," and then choose the "Export as PDF" option, as seen on the next page:

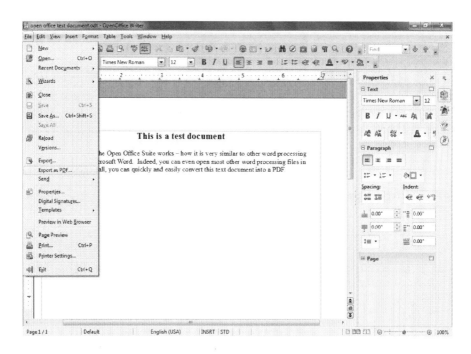

At this point, you'll get several options to choose from – the default options are fine, so you can skip over these options and click the "Export" button near the bottom.

Once you do that, the software will ask you to save the file in your chosen location using your chosen file name. Click save once you've entered your file name and location.

Step 4: Verify your PDF document.

Now go to the place where you saved your document on your hard drive, double click on the PDF file, and verify that everything looks good.

And that's all there is to it. Even if you don't have the budget for the professional tools like Adobe's PDF conversion tool, you can still make great PDFs… for free!

Okay, having taken a lengthy look at "packaging", let's spend some time talking about "pricing"…

Part 2: <u>PRICING</u>.

Over and over again, the same question comes up in regards to selling a special report: *how much should I charge for it?*

Having created and/or licensed, over 75 different special reports, products, services and other information based materials, I can say with great certainty…

I'm still <u>no expert</u> at pricing. ☺

There are all kinds of formulas for determining price that we won't go into because most are more confusing than they are useful. Let me sum up what I've learned in many years online – and what I go by in pricing my own materials. There are three simple "rules" that, to me, govern the amount you should charge for your special reports.

Rule #1 –

Your <u>content</u> is the most important factor in determining your price.

You can pretty much answer "*how much should I charge for it*" by answering "*how much is it worth?*"

<u>Think about it</u>: How much would YOU pay for 10 pages of a special report. Well, that depends, of course, on what the report is about. If it's 10 pages of "how to mud-wrestle an angry crocodile", then chances are you wouldn't pay much for the report. On the other hand, if the 10 pages contained a list of the next 20 winners of the World Series, the information would be quite valuable to you and the amount you'd spend for it would bear this out.

> Your content is the most important factor in determining your price. If you are a poor baseball player and demand a $20 million a year contract with the Yankees, you're out of luck because you can't deliver enough value. However, if you're the hottest free agent on the market and you demand that contract, you just might get it because you CAN bring that value to the table.

The point is this: How much you charge for your report is going to depend upon how good the report is. Can you deliver the goods?

Rule #2 –

Your competition's inadequacies help place a premium on your content.

Listen, if you've got something that works which others don't have, that's gonna have a big impact upon the price (and demand!) of your special report. Few people will buy a special report on something of interest to them if it's the same old thing they've already read a thousand times before. But, if you can prove that you know some secret, have some special insight, possess some short cut, can point to some advantage that your competition doesn't have, then your report's "value" just went up a few more notches.

What's missing from your competition's products and services that you have in your special report? Focus on that and you'll find customers focused on you!

Rule #3 –

Your customer's expectations, buying habits and desires make the final decision.

Ultimately, the "right price" is in the hands of your potential customers. They make the final decision as to whether or not they are willing to pay X price for your special report.

There are several different factors that influence their buying decisions including:

- What they reasonably expect to receive from your special report.

- What they are accustomed to paying for similar offers.

- How much of a desire they have for your special report at this time.

The good news is: You can, to some degree, have influence over all of this.

Now, having given you some considerations for pricing – these 3 "rules" – let me provide you with a VERY general "rule of thumb" when it comes to pricing your special report.

As a VERY general "rule of thumb", I price my special reports at around $0.75-$1.00 per page.

Length of Special Report	Price of Special Report
7-15 pages	$10.00
16-20 pages	$17.00
20-30 pages	$20.00

Anything more than 30 pages is no longer a special report, it's a product.

Now, again, if this is privileged information that has a much higher value, certainly your pricing would be different.

But, for most *"special reports"*, this is a good guideline to price by. Unless you have some significant reason to look at a different pricing structure, stick with this one.

Okay, one more thing we want to talk about in this segment, and that is *"positioning"*...

Now, before I begin talking about this aspect of your special report, let me say a word to those of you who might be beginners or relatively new to selling information. If anything I say in the next few minutes is confusing to you, just skip this section and don't worry about it right now. What we're about to talk about is "optional". It's a way to gain an edge, but if it's over your head, it's not important for you right now.

So, if any of this starts to make you wonder "how can I do this" or "I don't really understand", then just skip it and go on to the next segment on writing your mini-sales letter. It's not critical. It's just something I do need to discuss in order to be complete and help users at all levels of experience.

Part 3: <u>POSITIONING</u>.

Now, without delving too deep into *"positioning"* – which could be a rather lengthy discussion in itself – what I want to help you do is to develop what's known as a *"USP"* or *"unique sales proposition"*.

Defined: "Unique Sales Proposition"

An intentional, clearly visible means of separating yourself from others to create a competitive edge. It's what makes you different from others used as an advantage. What is it about you that's better than the rest stated in a way that engages prospects. That's your "*unique sales proposition*".

Let me tell you a story to illustrate this point to perfection...

I'll be the first to admit that I'm not in the greatest physical shape of my life. When I married my lovely wife 27 years ago, I had a 30 inch waste and weighed in at a whopping 165 pounds. I played basketball, tennis, biked and ran most days of the week and was on top of my game.

Something happened during the past 27 years. I developed a new hobby. It's called "*eating*." ☺

Recently, I decided it was time to tone up again. My goal is simple: to get back into good physical shape. At age 51, it's not going to be as easy as it was back at 24, but then again, I've always liked a good challenge.

So, for example, say you were out looking at equipment. You spot a shelf of "exercise balls." You know, the big bright blue balls that you inflate and do various exercises on." Having seen that they can be useful in toning abdominal muscles (which is where I want to start!), you decide to take a closer look.

Here's what you found -

> Four completely identical bright blue exercise balls. I'm talking the exact same size. The exact same yellow foot pump to inflate the ball. The exact same tube of glue to repair the ball should you decide to take a razor blade and slice it to bits after a few days. ☺

Three of the products sold for the exact same price of $12.99. The fourth product had an asking price of $16.99.

You immediately decided you would buy the $16.99 version.

Why spend more money for the exact same product? Here's why...

- Product A, B and C all had the standard product name of "*Brand A Exercise Ball*", "*Brand B Exercise Ball*" and "*Brand C Exercise Ball*". They all showed basically the same photographs of various exercises and the benefits were all basically the same.

- Product D was entitled -- get this -- "*Awesome Abs Exercise Ball*". And the exercises it showed were all designed to strengthen and tone abdominal muscles.

Same "*product*". Different "*focus.*" Game over.

There are <u>three lessons</u> to learn here...

Lesson #1: *"You can sell the same product at a higher price than your competition."* Delete this nonsense that says you should "undercut" your competitor in price to be successful. Not true. Lower price doesn't mean greater sales. To the contrary, you can actually RAISE YOUR PRICE and sell more than ever. And here's how...

Lesson #2: *"The key to selling at a higher price is POSITIONING."* It's all about how you PRESENT your offer. It's all about how you PACKAGE your offer. It's about your POSITION. A quarter pound hamburger will cost you $2 at McDonald's. They are "budget fast food". The same quarter pound hamburger will cost you over $10 bucks at Red Robin (they just opened up at my local mall, so I know). They bill themselves as offering "gourmet hamburgers". What's the difference? Position within the industry.

Lesson #3: *"An easy way to position for profits is to focus on a niche."* Jack Trout, the leading expert on positioning, has taught two things about positioning (actually, MANY things, but we'll narrow it down to two for now)...

1. It's better to be first in your people's mind than better.
2. If you can't be first in their minds in one category create a new category.

That's what "*Awesome Abs Exercise Ball*" did. It probably wasn't the first exercise ball on the market. But, it's the only exercise ball I've ever seen to this date that is focused on "*abdominal muscles*". It has positioned itself to focus on a NICHE market where it can be FIRST.

The bottom line is this...

You can SELL MORE if you POSITION yourself FIRST in a SPECIFIC NICHE market.

Now, what does all of that mean to you and your "*special report*"? Let's get personal here and talk about creating YOUR "*unique sales proposition*".

While there are many different aspects of developing a "USP", I want to look at the two easiest things you can do to develop your own presence and really separate yourself from your competition in an advantageous way.

(1) Focus on a specific <u>BENEFIT</u>. What is it that you've got which no one else does? Specifically, what about your special report makes it "*special*"? What's different? What's exclusive?

- Is it the only report available on the topic?
- Does it have more ideas than any other report?
- Have you broken things down into the easiest-to-follow steps?
- Does it include something that's missing from others?
- Is it written in a more "user-friendly" language?
- Does it include significantly helpful screenshots?
- Do you reveal some little known fact or secret strategy?
- Have you produced some staggering results?
- Is it a completely different approach to the subject?

- Does it contain the latest information or updated ideas?
- Does it disclose something that's "top secret"?
- Is it the most complete report available?
- Does it explain things in greater detail?
- Is it full of ways to apply existing information?
- Does it have brainstorming exercises?
- Does it include things like forms and worksheets?
- Is it specifically for "advanced users"?
- Does it expand upon an existing concept?
- Does it offer an easier or faster way to accomplish a task?
- Does it offer a different solution to a common problem?

I've just given you 20 different ways that your report can be "*positioned*" in a unique way. Surely there is something among the 20 questions that I've just asked to which you can respond with an emphatic "*yes*"!

Listen, you've got something in that special report that no one else has and that's what we need to determine. What is it about your special report that stands out among what others are offering?

Focus on that. This is going to be especially important in just a few minutes as we begin talking about your sales letter for the special report. Focus on a specific "benefit" to the reader – what can you offer them that no one else can?

And the second thing you can focus on is...

(2) Focus on a specific <u>CROWD</u>. That is, position your report for a specific demographic group. With this approach, the focus is less on WHAT you're teaching in the special report and more on WHO you're teaching it to.

(By the way, this is my course and I'll dangle my participles and use fragmented sentences if I want to. ☺ This is a perfect time for me to mention that – unless your special report is about grammar - most people don't care if you don't know your punctuation from your preposition.

It's all about your content.

It doesn't have to impress your high school English teacher. If your customers had wanted an eloquent work, they'd have ordered a poetry book instead of your report. And if you're one of those people who can't get past the fact that I put a comma in the wrong place or used the word "there" when it should have been "their", I would say to you … this isn't a homework assignment, so stop trying to grade it and focus on why you bought it in the first place – to LEARN SOMETHING. ☺)

Anyway, I digress. Back to the point: You can also focus on a specific "*crowd*" in order to position your special report. That's another aspect of what the "*Awesome Abs Ball*" folks did. They focused on a specific group of people: those wanting to tone up their abs.

You can do this too, in a couple of specific ways...

- **By Experience or Skill Level**. Focus your special report based on the experience level of others. In other words, your special report is specifically for "*beginners*" or specifically for "*advanced users*". Your special report is specifically for those who've achieved or not achieved a certain level of advancement.

Let me refer to a handful of examples.

Example 01: If you're writing a special report about "karate", it can be specifically targeted for "3rd degree black belts", for example. That's what makes you different ... while others might offer resources for ALL students of karate, yours is exclusively for those who've reached a certain level of experience.

Example 02: If you're writing a special report about "tennis shots", you could focus it specifically on those with a USTA rank of 3.5, which is the level of skill that I'm at. I'd be much more likely to buy something related to my skill level than a report for beginners or those who have mastered shots above my skill level.

Example 03: If you're writing a special report about "parenting", then you might position it specifically for "first-time" parents. Again, that makes you different.

Example 04: If you're writing a special report about "internet marketing", you might want to focus it on different qualifications of experience such as: for those who are beginners, for those who already have a website, for those without a list, for those who are already making $50K a year, etc.

So, that's one way of distinguishing yourself by targeting specific demographic groups based on "experience and skill levels".

- **By Distinction**. That is, by focusing on some "adjective" that describes a group of people. Again, here are some classic examples:

  Example 01: If you're writing a special report about "scrapbooking", then you could target it towards "Christian scrapbookers" with specific points and references of interest to believers in Jesus Christ.

  Example 02: If you're writing a special report about "fundraising", then you could target it towards "church groups" or "school groups" or "civic groups" or any other distinctive group of people who are interested in raising funds.

  Example 03: If you're writing a special report about "selling on Ebay®", you could focus it on "baseball card collectors", "antique dealers", "wholesalers" or any other distinctive group of people who might sell items at the online auction giant's website.

Example 04: If you're writing a special report about "saving your marriage" you could focus it specifically on "wives". And, to illustrate the point, let me say you could be even more selective by targeting "stay at home wives", "career wives" or "military wives".

The idea is find a distinctive group of people and target them with your special report. While most of your competition is catering to the masses, you've separated yourself by going after a slightly smaller demographic among the general audience.

Your special report is specifically for 3rd degree black belts, those who are having trouble losing that last 5 pounds, beginning internet marketers, Christian business owners, and school groups looking to raise funds.

So, that's how you can position your special report in order to make it more desirable to your potential customers and create an advantage over your competition.

Answer just two questions:

1. What does my special report offer that no one else does?

2. Who would my special report be just perfect for?

Obviously, the **best option** would be to position your report in both ways: by focusing on a specific benefit

<u>AND</u> a specific group, which is what the "*Awesome Abs*" folks did.

Okay, now with all of that in mind, let's move on to creating a mini-sales letter for your special report...

How To Create An Order-Producing Mini-Sales letter For Your Small Report

Once you finish writing and preparing your small report to sell online, it's time to shift your focus to the actual sales process.

And that process is going to begin with your "*mini-sales letter*".

I say "*mini*" sales letter because it's not important that you craft a 10-15 page direct response page like a full-length product would normally require. It shouldn't take as much persuasion to get others to buy a lower-priced offer as it would for a premium-priced offer.

So, we're going to talk about creating a shorter, yet equally as powerful, version of the internet sales letter. What I want to do is walk you through the construction of a sales letter from start to finish.

Everyone has their own way of developing a sales page, but the basic components are the same. And it is these basic components that I'm going to teach you in this segment.

> Sidebar: About WYSIWYG Software.
>
> Before we begin looking at the process of crafting a sales letter for your small report,

I need to mention that you'll need some kind of HTML software program in order to prepare your sales letter in the format of an HTML webpage for viewing online.

What I recommend is that you download a "WYSIWYG" editor, which means "what you see is what you get". This type of HTML editor doesn't require you to know anything about HTML coding. It's as simple as using your favorite word processor.

You have three basic options –

1. You can download free trial versions of many different WYSIWYG editors at Download.com or Tucows.com that will enable you to get a sales page created. I suggest you use the Coffee Cup editor, which works on both PCs and Macs. You can find it at www.coffeecup.com. Later on I'll give you a tutorial on how to use it.

2. You can purchase a copy of some of the better programs such as Dreamweaver or Microsoft Frontpage. If you have the money to spend, grab a new copy. Or, you can purchase earlier versions of these software programs at eBay.com for a significant discount.

3. You can hire someone to convert your written sales letter into a formatted HTML page by posting a project to Elance.com. You should be able to find someone to do this for you for $25-$30.

Having said all of that, let's begin looking at the process of writing a mini-sales letter to load to a website in order to get visitors to buy your small report.

As we make our way through the 11 basic parts of your mini-sales letter, I'll be referring to an example sales letter for this very product, "***How to Make A Small Fortune Online With Small Reports***", which is available for you to review at **http://www.SmallReportsFortuneMadeEasy.com** if you'd like to take a look as a guide for your own.

11 Parts Of An Order-Producing Special Report Mini-Sales Letter

1) Prehead. The first part of your sales letter is what's known as the "prehead". This is a short, introductory statement located at the very top of your sales page that is used to...

- ✓ Engage the reader's attention.
- ✓ Quickly introduce a key idea or qualification.
- ✓ Set the stage for the thrust of the sales message.

There isn't a set in stone rule for the length of a pre-headline. I've seen a prehead consisting of only one word – and I've seen a complete paragraph.

Here are some examples –

- (Mention A Specific Group) "Attention Bloggers, Article Writers, Information Publishers, Copywriters and

Anyone Else Who Writes Anything for His or Her Business…" (This is from ContentWritingMadeEasy.com.)

- (Mention A Specific Problem With Latest Development)
  "New Breakthrough Discovery For Arthritis Sufferers Shows..."

- (Mention A Credible Source)
  "As Seen On The Oprah Winfrey Show..."

- (Mention A Shocking Announcement)
  "You've Been Lied To About Teaching Qualifications!"

- (Mention A Statement Of Fact)
  "A Panel Of Top Experts Agree, This Is The Easiest Way To..."

If you look at my own mini-sales letter as a case study example, you'll find that I went with…

"It only takes 2-3 hours to create this cash cow…"

That short statement launches into my primary headline. But, before it does, it does a lot of valuable things for me as it conveys my message to the reader. It adequately gets their attention – what is this "cash cow" that can quickly be created? It introduces a key idea that I'll be expanding on later in the sales letter – "it only takes 2-3 hours". And, as we'll find out next, it seamlessly launches into my primary headline.

Speaking of which, that's the second "part" of your sales letter that we want to direct our attention to next...

2) Primary head. This is your main headline – located at the top center of your sales page immediately below your prehead. It should be in **larger, bolder** print and may contain certain words highlighted in different colored text for emphasis.

This is your biggest weapon of the sales page and should be used to showcase your biggest benefit to the reader.

> ➤ What is the ultimate "best reason" someone should buy your special report?
> ➤ What is the most desirable result of buying your report to the reader?
> ➤ What, above everything else, would be most beneficial about buying it?

This is your chance to quickly encapsulate your entire sales letter in one, eye-catching sentence that is GUARANTEED to be read by the visitor to your site.

Fire your biggest gun!

Now there are a lot of different models, templates and "*kinds*" of headlines that have been repeatedly used over the years which have proven to be very effective in producing orders.

I can't possibly cover them all, but what I want to share with you is one of my favorites that has really **generated great results** for me – and my clients – every time we've used it.

I call if "*If You Can, Then You Can*" model.

The idea is to make a simple, reasonable qualification that the reader must meet (that's the "if you can" part) in order to reap some tremendous result (that's the "then you can" part) of great interest to them.

Here's an example from my own mini-sales letter...

"IF YOU CAN WRITE 7-15 PAGE REPORTS, THEN YOU CAN
MAKE A LIVING ONLINE WORKING JUST <u>A FEW HOURS</u>
EACH WEEK FROM THE COMFORT OF YOUR HOME!"

As with any type of advertisement or sales copy, there are some simple things you'll want to make sure you do in creating your headline...

✓ **Use <u>Particulars</u>**. The more specific you can be, the better. Not only does your statement seem more believable with specifics, but in many instances it can see more reachable. It's not just "write reports", it's "write 7-15 page reports".

✓ **Use <u>Periods</u>.** One of the things most people want is a "time frame". How long will this take? When can I expect results? It's not just "make a living online working from home", it's "make a living working JUST A FEW HOURS each week..."

✓ **Use <u>Pictures</u>.** Unless they're a glutton for taking the road less traveled, most people want the easiest route to their destination of choice. Use word pictures to describe the ultimate result most desirable to the reader. It's not just "working from home", it's "working from the comfort of your home".

So, there's a lot to convey in your headline. It sets the tone for your entire sales message, so spend some time developing it based on the things we've talked about here.

I suggest you brainstorm at least a half a dozen different headlines.

You can even use these additional templates to help you find the best headline for your needs. Take note that for each of the templates below, I've provided two examples. The first is an example of how to use this headline for my product at www.contentwritingmadeeasy.com – in other words, I'm showing you that you can use each of these headlines for the same product. The second example shows you how to use the headline template in different niches. Check it out:

1. "At Last, Now You Too Can Discover the Secret of [Getting Some Benefit]!"

Examples:

- "At Last, Now You Too Can Discover the Secret of Creating High Quality Content Quickly and Easily Using Contentaire – Even If You Don't Consider Yourself a Writer!"

- "At Last, Now You Too Can Discover the Secret of Turning Back the Hands of

Time With This Amazing Anti-Aging
Regimen!"

2. "Who Else Wants [Specific Benefit]?"

Examples:

- "Who Else Wants to Create Content
  Effortlessly?"

- "Who Else Wants to Add 25 Yards to
  Their Golf Drives?"

3. "Here's the Quick and Easy Way to [Get Some Benefit]…"

Examples:

- "Here's the Quick and Easy Way to
  Create Sales Letters, Articles, Emails
  and All the Other Content You'll Ever
  Need…"

- "Here's the Quick and Easy Way to
  Housetrain Your Puppy…"

4. "How to [Start] [Get a Benefit] in as Little as [Short Time Period] From Now!"

Examples:

- "How to Start Creating High-Response
  Sales Letters, Engaging Articles and
  Profit-Pulling Emails in as Little as
  15 Minutes From Now!"

- "How to Lose 10 Pounds, Turn Heads and Start Feeling Great in as Little as One Short Month From Now!"

5. "What If [You Got Some Amazing Result]?"

Examples:

- "What if Every Sentence You Write Could Almost Effortlessly and Magically Form on Your Computer?"

- "What if You Gazes In the Mirror and Discovered You Looked 10 Years Younger?"

6. "How [Type of People Just Like You] Are [Getting Great Results] – And How You Can Too!"

Examples:

- "How Small Business Owners and Content Publishers Just Like You Are Creating High-Quality, Effective Sales Letters, Blog Posts, Emails and Other Content in a Fraction of the Time – And How You can Too!"

- "How Busy Moms Just Like You Are Homeschooling Their Children and Getting Them Into the Best Colleges in the Nation – And How You Can Too!"

7. "If You've Ever Wanted [Some Great Result], Then [Reader Needs to Take This Step...]"

Examples:

- "If You've Ever Wanted to Create More High-Quality Content for Your Business in a Fraction of the Time, Then You Need To Read This Important Announcement…"

- "If You've Ever Wanted to Become a Bestselling Author, Then You Need to Drop What You're Doing and Read This Exciting Letter…"

8. "Imagine [Getting Some Great Result]…"

Examples:

- "Imagine Creating Sizzling Sales Letters, Engaging Articles and Profit-Pulling Emails Simply by Filling in a Few Blanks on a Template…"

- "Imagine Seeing Your Name on the New York Times Bestseller List…"

9. "Here's a Little-Known Way to [Get a Benefit]…"

Examples:

- "Here's a Little Known Way to Quickly and Easily Create All the Content You Need for Your Business… Even if You Flunked High School English!"

- "Here's a Little-Known Way to Rid Your Garden of Pests Without Using Harmful Pesticides or Other Dangerous Toxins…"

10. "When [Type of Expert] Want [Some Type of Result], Here's What They Do…"

Examples:

- "When Professional Copywriters Want to Create High Response, Mouthwatering Sales Letters, Here's What They Do…"

- "When Personal Trainers Want to Get Beach Ready Abs Fast, Here's What They Do…"

By simply making some appropriate substitutions into any of the templates above, you should be able to craft an attention-grabbing start to your mini-sales letter.

Moving on, the next "part" I want to mention is the…

3) Posthead. This is similar to the "prehead" in that it's a brief connecting statement. This time, it bridges the gap from the headline to the opening paragraph of your copy.

Now, again, there are a lot of different usage ideas here as to what you should do with your posthead. I'm not a Dan Kennedy, Yanik Silver, Michel Fortin or some other world-class copywriter. But I am pretty good at convincing people to buy my courses, so let me tell you how I use a posthead on my own sales pages.

There are a couple of things that have proven to be effective that I want to mention -

- **Make A Statement Of Emphasis**. In other words, briefly expand upon what you said in the headline – but emphasize something that will make it even EASIER or FASTER or MORE REWARDING than what you've already stated. Here's what I went with in my posthead...

"Play Golf, Spend Time With Your Family Or Just Relax
With All Of Your Extra Time While Orders Come In Automatically!"

I chose to emphasize the "end result" the reader can be experiencing by following my instructions.

I could just as have easily stressed a way things will be made easier such as...

"Heck, I'll Even Show You How To Get Other People To Write The Reports For You!"

Or, I could have chosen to focus on "speeding up" the process by promising...

"Update: My New Bonus Chapter Shows You

***How To Get Your First Sale By Tomorrow
Afternoon!"***

The point is the same in all regards: the posthead is used to place emphasis on an easier, faster or more rewarding aspect of what I'm about to share in my letter to the reader.

- **Mention A Deadline Or Limit**. Another good use of your posthead is to begin creating urgency by stressing some kind of deadline or limit that you are imposing. A few examples include...

    ***"Only 50 Lucky Charter Members Will Be
    Accepted!"***
    ***"80% Off Introductory Price Ends On
    October 12th at Midnight!"***
    ***"There Are Just 24 16 Copies Left Before
    We'll Be Sold Out!"***

    Obviously, you'd give extensive details on this deadline or limit later towards the conclusion of your sales letter, but this is a great place to introduce some (legitimate!) deadline or limit that the reader needs to be aware of.

Once you have a posthead in place, you're ready to dive into the main body of your sales letter, beginning with your opening paragraph which includes...

4) Problem. Virtually every good sales letter begins – in one form or another – with an introduction of a problem.

- You're not getting enough traffic to your site.
- Your list isn't big enough.
- You still haven't dropped that last 10 pounds.
- Your spouse is wanting a divorce.
- You can't seem to manage your time.
- You're not as good at tennis as you'd like to be.
- You'd like the flexibility of working from home.
- You're really interested in homeschooling.
- You could be happier if just one thing changed.

Serious or trivial, stated positively or negatively, real or imagined, problems are the universal driving force behind many – if not most - decisions we make. We want to avoid them, correct them, minimize them or make up for them, but make no mistake about it, they have great influence in our lives.

We'd be happier without problems, or so we think. We'd at least try to give it a try. ☺ And, if we can't completely eliminate our problems, it sure would be nice to have something really wonderful happening in our lives that would diminish or overshadow them. We all have things that we'd like to improve upon. Things we'd like to see changed to some degree. Things we'd like to make better.

So, one of the **best ways** you can begin your mini-sales letter is to establish the fact that there is a *problem* that needs to be addressed. Generally, by telling some kind of story that allows you to identify with the reader and the problem they face.

Here's an excerpt of part of the opening for my mini-sales letter for the *"How to Make A Small Fortune Online With Small Reports"* course...

```
------------------------

You've probably figured it out by now:
"certain" people seem to be making all
the money because of a "buddy system" in
place where they all promote each other's
products.

Chances are you're not in their club,
right?

You're busy promoting their affiliate
program and not the other way around.
You're busy buying their latest offer
while they haven't spent a penny with
you.  You're still working a "real job"
40+ hours a week while they're off
playing golf - and they're spending your
hard earned money to pay their green
fees!

Listen, I know - it's frustrating on the
outside looking in.  I hear ya.

But, what if I could change all of that
for you?

------------------------
```

See how a problem was presented here? See how I
identified, even empathized with the reader? And see
how I hinted at the ability to make a positive change
for her?

Let me give you a template you can use…

```
--------------------------

Have you ever noticed how some people
make it look so easy to [get some benefit
or result, like lose weight, make money,
etc]?

Then you try to do the same thing, and
you just end up [getting some bad
result].  It's frustrating because [list
reasons why it's frustrating]. Seems like
you just can't [get a benefit or result],
because [reason why they can't do it].

Listen, I know what it's like, because I
used to [describe how you used to have
the same problem]. And it's not your
fault.  It's just that [reason why it's
not their fault, such as no one ever
taught them the right way to do it].

All that changes right now…

--------------------------
```

It's an easy transition from here to the next "part" of the mini-sales letter

5) Product. Now that you've established a problem, it's time to share the solution – namely, what <u>YOU</u> have to offer in your "*small report*"!

Here's where you let loose with the "*unique sales proposition*" we talked about earlier.

> ***"You know how others _____,
> well here's what I do that's different…"***

Without being arrogant or prideful, it's time to **talk about yourself**: your experiences, your knowledge, your secret weapon, your special way of doing things.

- ✓ Explain what you have to offer in your small report that will help the reader to solve the problem they are facing.

- ✓ Tell a story to explain HOW you found out what you'll be sharing in our special report.

- ✓ Empathize with the reader – you've been where they were and look at how things have changed since you made your discovery of "what works".

- ✓ Point out what makes you different than the rest of those out there who might be offering similar products.

- ✓ Refer to tips, strategies, practices, etc. that you reveal in your special report (without telling them exactly WHAT those items are, of course!)

- ✓ Mention specific results you've achieved by using the information included in your special report.

Let me give you a template you can use for this section...

Introducing [name of report], a [number]-page report that's jam-packed with everything you need to know to [get some good result or benefits].

You know how others [do something the same way]? Well, here's what I do different: [quick summary of your USP].

You see, it didn't take me long to realize that those other solutions don't work all that well because [list common weakness or flaw of other products, but don't mention specific products]. That's why I decided to [describe in more detail how your product is different – why it works better].

It worked – and it worked really well.

[Describe how it worked for you – share specific results.]

That's no fluke. I then tested this strategy with others, and they got the same results as I did. For example, [share a quick story about someone who got great results with your information].*

Listen, this [type of] strategy worked for me, it's worked for countless others, and it will work for you too so that you can finally [get some great result].

----

* When you start talking about results, don't just make claims, PROVE them. Which brings us up to "part" 6, which is your "proof"...

6) Proof. Anyone can make claims about what they've done and what they know, but how many can prove it? And, when they prove it, how much more effective is their claim?

> People, in general, are naturally skeptical. Especially those who've been around the block and have fallen for hype before. If you want to bridge the gap between their wallet and your order button, you've got to establish trust.

And the surest way to establish trust is to prove what you're saying is true.

There are three simple things you can do to validate your claims by providing a form of evidence that I want to quickly point out...

1. **PROVIDE a testimonial**. It's one thing when YOU say the information included in your special report works...it's another thing entirely for someone else to proclaim that they've duplicated or exceeded your results by trying the information themselves. A testimonial from someone who's read, used and seen results from your special report represents a voice of credibility speaking on your behalf. One or two testimonials should be sufficient for your special report mini-sales letter.

2. **POINT to visual evidence**. What diet program appears more legit than the one with a "before and after" photo of someone who's lost weight? When you can provide screenshots, photographs or other "visual" evidence to substantiate your

claims, it can go a long way to tear down the wall of reluctance that rests between you and your potential customer.

3. **<u>POSE</u> a challenge**. If possible, get the reader of your mini-sales letter to do something themselves to test your validity. When I was selling a course on "viral ebooks", I would have folks go to Google.com and do a search for my name to PROVE I knew how to get free ebooks distributed to tens of thousands of website. It's not always possible, but if it is, posing a challenge for the reader to do something to test you is a nice option.

When you've laid out your "proof", it's time to get specific about what's included in your special report...

7) Points. Using a "*bulleted list*" of benefit points is one of the most effective ways to really drive home the "*reason why*" the reader would want to purchase your special report. It also allows you the opportunity to address **several different "angles"** of the information you include – one of which might be that special "hot button" with the reader that seals the deal.

You've seen them on just about every sales letter.

Three quick things I want to mention about these "points"...

- **Stress benefits, NOT features**. The classic statement about benefits vs. features is this: "no one cares about your lawn mower, they only care about their lawn". Your special report might very well have 10 ready-made lesson plans included ... but what does it mean to the reader? It means they don't have to spend time developing the lesson plans themselves; it means they don't have to be in a rush; it means they can use their saved time doing something more enjoyable. A benefit is simply WHY the reader should care about your feature.

- **Stress particulars, NOT generalities**. It's not "Helpful ways to...", it's "11 helpful ways to...". It's not "lose weight", it's "lose 7 pounds in 2 weeks". The more specific you can be, the better. And, let me mention something that really adds credibility to your bullet points is to list a specific PAGE in which the information is found in your special report. What I do is write something like (Page 7) – separated by parenthesis – after the bullet point so the reader can know exactly where to find what I've mentioned in that point. Very, very effective.

- **Stress majors, NOT minors.** You should only use about 6 or 7 bullet points for a "mini-sales letter" – so make them count. You want to stress the most desirable benefits to the reader ... the "major" helps included in your special report. It's important that you fire your biggest guns. And try to focus on different aspects of the information you're sharing in the special report.

> Example: One bullet point might focus on the "quickness" of forthcoming results, while another bullet point might focus on the

"ease" of forthcoming results, while another bullet point might focus on the "responses of others" in relation to the forthcoming results, etc.

As you can tell, bullet points are really similar to headlines in that they focus on showing your readers the benefits of your product.

As such, you can use the previous headline templates to create your bullet points too, plus you can use these additional six templates:

1. "Here's a stunningly simple way to [get a benefit] – see page [number]!"

Example: "Here's a stunning simple way to get firmer abs – see page 10!"

2. "What does [one seemingly related thing] have to do with [getting a benefit]? You'll find out on page [number]!"

Example: "What does a piece of aluminum foil have to do with you looking ten years younger? You'll find out on page 22!"

3. "If you want [benefit or result], then you'll love the secret [type] strategy revealed on page [number]!"

Example: "If you want to get rid of slugs in your garden once and for all, then

you'll love the secret slug-trapping
strategy revealed on page 3!"

4. "You'll discover the #1 way to [get a benefit] – you'll wish you had known about this years ago!"

Example: "You'll discover the #1 way to
get rid of belly fat – you'll wish you
had known about this years ago!"

5. "You'll find out the best way to [get a benefit] – it's easier than you think!"

Example: "You'll find out the best way to
shave three strokes off your golf game –
it's easier than you think!"

6. See page [number] to find out a surprising way to [get benefit]... even if [you don't have some prerequisite]!"

Example: "See page 22 to find out a
surprising way to get your business
website up and running today – even if
you don't know HTML from a bar of soap!"

Now, after you've got 6-7 bullet points in place here,
it's time for the next "part" of your mini-sales letter,
which is your...

8) Pull.   That is, your "call to action". You know the
drill from every commercial advertisement you've
seen on television...

> ***"Operators are standing by ... place your order
> NOW!"***

Don't delay. Quantities are limited. The next 10 callers get xyz. Yada, yada, yada. Blah, blah, blah. Reminds me of the teacher on the Charlie Brown cartoons: "waaa, waaa, waaa, waaa, waaaa."

> While I'm certainly not a believer in using psychological mind games to prey on the emotions of readers to push them over the edge, it is important that you point them towards a decision. It is important that you instruct them to take advantage of your offer and place their order.

Now, every good copywriter will tell you: it's all about creating urgency. In other words, you don't want them to delay in making the decision to buy ... they might not ever be back again. ***You've got their attention RIGHT NOW, so you want them to make their decision RIGHT NOW***.

Perhaps the best way to get them to do this is to impose some kind of deadline or limit which makes it necessary to order soon in order to take advantage of a special price, extra incentive or availability.

- **Special Price.** By offering a discount to all who purchase within a specific period of time (or to a selected number of people who order ... I.E. The first 100), you can create a sense of urgency. This isn't going to be as useful to you as a writer of low-priced special reports simply because, let's face it, the difference between the "regular" price of $15 and the "discount price" of $10 isn't substantial enough to be alluring.

> Example: order now and you can take advantage of the introductory price of this report of just $10 – that's a 50% discount off the regular price!

- **Extra Incentive.** You may want to consider offering an additional bonus (we'll talk more about this in an upcoming section) to those who order within a specified time or specific number. This CAN be an effective option for you to use. For example: If your special report is about "setting up a mini-sales letter" you might state, "The first 100 people who order will receive a free copy of a legal disclaimer you can use on your website to protect you from FTC lawsuits and seizures..."

- **Availability.** Another option is to remove the special report from circulation after a specified date or a specified number of units is sold. I don't like this one for obvious reasons: I'd like to sell as many copies as I can sell!

  However, one strategy that I do see merit in using is taking a special report "off the market" for an unspecified period of time. In other words, you "retire" the report for several months and then bring it back later – or even add more information to it and convert it into a larger product.

  Or, another idea is to no longer make it available from your website and only offer it as a backend to a second report you create later, etc.

Still another idea is to create a bonus offer that is ONLY available for a limited time or in limited quantities.

> Example: "Be one of the next 97 people to order now, and you'll also get [specifics of bonus] absolutely free!"

Now, a limit or deadline isn't as necessary for low-cost special reports as they are for full-scale, premium-priced products … so don't waste a lot of time on this.

I will give you three age-old, still-effective ways to "encourage" people to order in your call to action that have "built-in" urgency:

1. The Rule of <u>RESULTS</u>. Stated simply, "the longer you wait to get started, the longer it will be before you see results". The flipside is also true: "the quicker you get started, the quicker you'll see results".

> Example: "So order now… because the sooner you do, the sooner you'll fit into your skinny jeans again!"

2. The Rule of <u>RESPONSE</u>. There is much information that isn't as effective as more people begin using it. This is especially true of "marketing" or "business" information.

> Example: "Order now to gain the edge on your competitors – you'll kick yourself if you don't get this report today!"

3. The Rule of <u>RESTRICTION</u>. There are many times when a delay in buying and applying information restricts the reader in what they can accomplish.

Example: "Time is running out! If you want to take advantage of the Christmas rush, then you need to get your website up and running today. So click here to order now while there's still time to get your business ready for Christmas!"

By using these three "built-in" triggers to create urgency, you can reasonably point your site visitors to a buying decision without resorting to high-pressure sales tactics.

Speaking of pressure – your next "part" of the mini-sales letter certainly helps remove it...

9) Promise. In other words, your "*guarantee*". Risk reversal is the ultimate way to remove any remaining barriers between you and your potential customer. Make it clear that THEY have "nothing to risk". If they are dissatisfied for any reason, you'll refund their money with no hassles.

Note: It's important that you include any "terms" relevant to your guarantee. For example: how long does the customer have in order to obtain a refund should they choose to do so? In many cases, it's the law to provide at least 30 days. And, depending upon whom you choose to process your orders, there will be requirements from those companies that

you'll need to comply with. We'll talk
more about that later.

The important thing is that you communicate to your
site visitors that you are committed to their absolute
satisfaction.

Ultimately, they only pay for what they are pleased
with having bought.

Again, let me give you a quick look at my own
guarantee...

But, what you won't have is your month back.

The point is this: you can start today with nothing and in a month have several small reports (perhaps even your first bundle if you want!) live and taking orders. Or, you can NOT order the course, come back in a month and be no better off than you were today.

That's not a sales tactic, that's reality.

So, go ahead and order today. I'll make sure you are satisfied or give your money back. There's no risk...

All You Need To Do Is Email Me And I'll
Give Your Money Back If You're Not Satisfied...

How about a money-back guarantee?

Here it is: You've got sixty days to use the course to see if it works for you. If you're not thoroughly satisfied, then you can simply email me and I'll give your full purchase price back to you.

It's that simple. No questions asked. No hassles. No delays. I'll send it back to you just as quickly as you sent it to me. That seems only fair.

Let me give you a template you can use to create your
own guarantee. Simply tweak this to fit your needs:

Your Satisfaction is 100% Guaranteed!

Download [Name of Report] right now, and
you'll have a full [number] [time frame,
such as days/weeks/months] to read every

page of the report and use every strategy
to [get some benefit].

If you're not absolutely satisfied for
any reason, and if you don't agree that
this is the best way to [get a benefit],
simply contact me by [instructions for
what to do, such as email you or contact
your help desk] within [length of
guarantee period] and I'll promptly and
cheerfully refund every penny.

No questions, no quibbles, no hoops to
jump through... so order now risk free!

And with that...

10) Process. Finally, you're ready to take orders and
start making money! (Congratulations, by the way! ☺)
You'll want to include three simple things here in this
order process that are worth mentioning...

✓ **Last-Minute Instructions**. Let them know
   how the order will be fulfilled (I.E. "Instant
   download" or "shipped within 24 hours", etc.)
   Mention any bonuses they'll receive. If there
   are any special instructions (I.E. Register for
   free updates on the download page, etc.) then
   mention those as well.

✓ **Links**. That is, your order link(s). I usually
   have the link read something like "Click Here to
   Order Now" or "Get Instant Access By Clicking
   Here" or some similar statement. Obviously, the
   actual link itself will need to lead to an order

processor to accept payment on your behalf. This link will be provided by whatever processor you use to handle your orders ... which we'll talk about in our next section.

✓ **Legalities**. Always, always, always include appropriate legal statements to protect yourself. Many have turned to internet law attorney, Bob Silber, to create their own disclaimer, terms of service, legal disclaimer and privacy notice. They have had to pay a rather large sum to have these created for their own use, but I believe he has an option available now where you can pay a monthly fee for use of legal documents he creates on your behalf. You can Visit http://www.attorneybobsilber.com for more information. Of course, you can also obtain legal forms from other sources, just make sure you have some kind of disclaimers in place to protect yourself. A popular option that many people use is http://www.Autoweblaw.com

So, here's what the "order process" portion of the sales letter can look like...

And that brings us to the final "part" of your mini-sales letter...

11) Postscript. Immediately below your name at the bottom of your sales page should be a "postscript". You know the drill, "P.S. Blah, Blah, Blah".

Why include a P.S.?

Because people <u>WILL</u> read them. Sometimes they'll even jump to the bottom of the page and **read that first**. (They're usually looking for the price.) Regardless of the order in which they get there, *they will get there*. And they'll read your P.S.

So, since you're gonna have their attention at this point, it's important that you *make the most of it*.

Three powerful ways to finish strong in the sales process is to use your postscript to "*recap*", "*remind*" or "*reinforce*"...

1. <u>RECAP</u> the offer. That is, in ONE sentence, give a brief account of what the reader will be receiving when they place their order.

   Example #1: "P.S. This is a no-brainer: you'll get 3 years of homeschooling research boiled down to 12 pages of 'no-fluff' content in detailed, step-by-step format for only $10.")

   Example #2: "P.S. Order now and you'll get instant access to [name of report] plus [name of any bonuses, if applicable], all for the low price of just [$ price]. So order now, because [give a benefit]!"

2. <u>REMIND</u> them of a key benefit. Take a sentence to point out once again a desirable result the reader can be experiencing by making the purchase.

   Example #1: "P.S. Don't forget, in less than 24 hours you can actually see your first order ... isn't that exciting!?")

   Example #2: "P.S. You won't find a better way to [get some benefit] and [get some other benefit], so order now!"

3. <u>REINFORCE</u> the call to action. Did you impose a deadline or limit? Did you

mention an extra incentive? Did you pose a challenge? Use your "postscript" to reinforce some element of your call to action.

Example #1: "P.S. Unfortunately, when the remaining 17 copies are gone, this offer won't be repeated. Order now."

Example #2: "P.S. Remember, if you order now you'll also get instant access to [name of bonus product] – but hurry, this special offer ends [list when it ends].

Now let's pull all these pieces together to create your sales letter. Here's a template you can use...

To Anyone Who Wants [to Achieve a Specific Result]...

"Now You Too Can [Get a Big Benefit] and [Get Another Big Benefit] – Even If You [Don't Have Some Prerequisite]!"

You're about to discover the same [type of/topic] secret the pros use to [get a benefit] – you won't believe how well it works! Read on...

Dear [Type of Person, such as "Fellow Small Business Owner"],

Seems like everywhere you turn, people are [getting some great result]. They all make it look so easy. But when you try to do the same thing, you end up [describe the poor result people typically get].

It's frustrating. You're tired of [being in some negative position]. You just want [to get some good result]. You'd love if you could only [get some other benefit or good result].

Good news...

Now You Can [Get a Great Benefit] in as Little as [Some Short Time Period From Now]!

Introducing [name of your short report], which is your complete guide to [completing some step-by-step process or getting some result], [getting some other benefit] and [getting a third big benefit]!

Inside this exciting [number of page] page jam-packed report, you'll discover:

- A quick and easy way to [get a result] – see page [number] for the exciting details!
- You'll discover a surprising way to [get a benefit] – and it has nothing to do with [what the reader expects it has to do with]!

- You'll find out how to [get a benefit], even if you [don't have some skill, experience, background, possession, etc] – see page [number]!

- Can't [get some benefit] – you'll find out a surefire method for [getting this result] on page [number]!

- You'll get a surprisingly simple [number]-step process for [getting a result] – [getting a specific benefit] has never been so easy!

- You'll find out how the pros [get some specific result] – see page [number] for this little-known strategy they hoped you'd never find out!

And much more. By the time you've finished this report, you'll know exactly how to [get a benefit] and [get another benefit]!

But don't take my word for it. Just see what others are saying about this eye-opening report:

[Insert testimonials here –
bold or otherwise emphasize some of the best parts of the testimonials. Choose strong testimonials, such as ones that talk about what results they've received.]

[You can also insert other forms of proof here, such as before and after photos.]

So let me ask you a question: Are YOU ready to [get some benefit]?

Then order [name of report] risk-free today!

It doesn't matter if [you've tried and failed before]. It doesn't matter if [you don't have some prerequisite]. It doesn't even matter if [you don't have some other prerequisite]. Because when you know the secret [type of] strategy revealed inside this report, you'll know exactly how to [get a big benefit]!

Best of all, you too can discover these secrets today for just [low price]. That's less than the cost of small pizza. You won't find a better deal around, so order risk free today…

Your Satisfaction is Guaranteed!

Download [Name of Report] right now, and you'll have a full [number] [time frame, such as days/weeks/months] to read every page of the report and use every strategy to [get some benefit].

If you're not absolutely satisfied for any reason, and if you don't agree that this is the best way to [get a benefit], simply contact me by [instructions for what to do, such as email you or contact your help desk] within [length of guarantee period] and I'll promptly and cheerfully refund every penny.

No questions, no quibbles, no hoops to jump through… so order now risk free!

[If you have any bonuses, list them here]

We both know this is a great deal, so…

Place Your Order Below Now to Get Started

Get out your credit card and click the "buy now" button below to place your order. Once you do, you'll get instant access to a downloadable .PDF file that's readable on any PC, Mac or even on your mobile device.

[Quickly remind them of anything else included in the offer, such as bonus gifts.]

So order now, because the sooner you do, the sooner you'll start enjoying [some benefit]

[Insert order button or form]

[Insert legal links as needed]

[Insert your signature]

P.S. Simply put, this is the quickest, easiest and smartest way to [get a specific result]. So don't waste another moment trying to [get some result on your own or trying faulty methods] – order [name of report] right now and you could be [getting some specific result] in as little as [short time frame] from now! Click here to get started – you'll be glad you did!

All right, you've just been given a crash course in copywriting! If you make your way through these 11 "parts" of your mini-sales letter, you should have a nice piece in place soon to convince visitors to your site to buy your special report.

Now, once you've actually written the words for your sales letter, what you need to do is create an .html file. This is the file you'll load up to your website so that your visitors will be able to see your sales letter

Speaking of your site, it's time to look at how to set it up so you can actually start taking orders. Let's identify some things you can do to get that in the works...

How To S.E.T.U.P.™ A Web Site To Sell Your Special Report

It's getting exciting now, isn't it?

You've finished your report by this time. You've written your sales letter. It's time. It's time to get things setup at your own site to begin taking orders.

So, that's what we're going to focus on for the next few minutes.

Now, let me preface the training that I'm about to give you by saying that it's "*impossible*" for me to explain everything to you in step-by-step format. There are just too many **variables** that are different for each situation based on choices that you make from this point on.

Let me offer an example –

> Example: There are dozens of different options for who you choose to process your orders. I couldn't possibly give you a universal "step-by-step" look at processing your orders because the manner in which things are done at each processor is going to be different. I.E. I couldn't say, "Login to your control panel and click on the NEW PRODUCT link". That would help you if you choose to work with Processor A, but would totally confuse you if you went with Processor B because the interface is completely different.

However, while I do leave the final decisions up to you, what I'm going to do is give you one recommendation for each resource — and then I'll give you instructions or even a tutorial for how to accomplish a task using that particular resource.

If you choose a different resource, the underlying idea will be the same, though the exact instructions may differ. Nonetheless, these instructions should equip you to actually get it done regardless of the choices you make.

Sound fair?

Good. Let's get started...

How To S.E.T.U.P.™ A Web Site To Sell Your Special Report

I use an acronym (S.E.T.U.P.) to explain the five steps for preparing your web site to sell your special reports...

```
S - SELECT a domain name.
E - ESTABLISH web site hosting.
T - THINK about the order process.
U - UPLOAD your files.
P - PREPARE for your first order.
```

Let's take a closer look at each of these five steps...

1) SELECT a domain name. The process of setting up your web site begins with selecting your own domain name. The price for registering a domain name is less than $10 per year at most registrars (I'll give you a recommendation in a moment), so it's not going to cost you much to get this done.

The key is to select the appropriate domain name. There are four characteristics of a good domain name for your small report that I want to quickly mention...

✓ **Only choose a .com domain name**. There are a gazillion different extensions available these days, but the primary one remains ".com". Unless there is a significant reason to do something else, I'd only recommend you choose a .com domain name.

✓ **Make your domain name easy to remember**. Keep it as short as possible. Avoid dashes. Avoid numeric substitutions. (I.E. ILive4Weekends.com) Look for domain names that are short and easy to spell and you'll be in good shape.

✓ **If possible, focus on keywords.** I don't spend a lot of time analyzing search engine optimization tricks and tactics, but if I don't have to go out of my way to work things in my favor I certainly don't mind being smart. In some instances you might get ranked higher in searches at some engines for some of the words in your domain name. For example: You'd have a better chance at getting ranked higher for "television sets" if your domain name was "BuyCheapTelevisionSetsOnline.com" than if it was "GetANewUnit.com".

✓ **Choose a "matching" domain name**. That is, choose a domain name that is directly related to the title of your special report. In my own example of "*How To Make A Small Fortune Online With Small Reports*", I chose "SmallReportsFortuneMadeEasy.com". Notice that it meets all of these criteria.

Okay, so let me give you 15 domain templates you can use to help brainstorm your own domain name:

1. [keyword]101

> Example: DogTraining101

2. [keyword]Online

> Example: BloggingOnline

3. Best[keyword]Ideas

> Example: BestOrganicGardeningIdeas

4. [keyword]Center

> Example: BodybuildingCenter

5. [keyword]For[Group]

> Example: GolfForBeginners

6. [keyword]Tips

Example: TrophyFishingTips

7. [keyword]Secrets

Example: WeightLossSecrets

8. [keyword]University

Example: ChildRearingUniversity

9. [keyword]Reports

Example: SmallBusinessReports

10. AllAbout[keyword]

Example: AllAboutStockTrading

11. [keyword]TipsAndTricks

Example: CandleMakingTipsAndTricks

12. [keyword]Information

Example: CarRestorationInformation

13. [keyword]MadeEasy

Example: MarathonTrainingMadeEasy

14. Amazing[keyword]

Example: AmazingAntiAging

15. Surefire[keyword]

Example: SurefireWeightLoss

Here are two important points:

1. What I want you to do is brainstorm several possible domain names *BEFORE* you ever visit a registrar. That's because there is a good chance that your "first choice" domain name—and maybe even your second, third, fourth and fifth choices—have already been registered. As such, you'll want to go to the registrar with a list of possible names in hand, so that you can quickly go through your list of possibilities until you find one that's available.

2. The second thing I want you to know is that you should NOT do any searching at a domain registrar until you have your credit card in hand and are ready to buy a domain on the spot. Many people have expressed disappointment when they've searched for a domain, found it available, but didn't buy it at that moment. Then hours or days later they went back only to discover someone else had already purchased the domain.

In some cases, this happens because certain domain registrars seem to make their search results available. That means that people can see what others are searching for—and if the searchers don't buy an available domain name, someone else might come along and snap it up.

In other cases, it's simply a coincidence. I know I've merely thought about a domain name before—didn't search for it anywhere—and when I went to register it, I was disappointed to find someone else had registered it just a day or two ago.

Point is, do NOT search until you're ready to buy. And once you find a domain name available, *buy it immediately*. Don't even wait a few minutes—snap it up before someone else does.

Now, there are many, many "*registrars*" online where you can pay to register a domain name for your exclusive use. However, what you want to do is choose a registrar with a good reputation, good support documentation, good customer service and good prices.

One of my personal favorites that meets all these requirements is GoDaddy.com. I have personally purchased over 2,000 domain names from GoDaddy. I admit. I have a problem. ☺

If you don't already have a domain name registrar that you use, then I suggest you use GoDaddy.com as well.

Registering a domain name on GoDaddy.com is really simple. All you have to do is go to www.godaddy.com, and enter your desired domain name in the form at the top of the page, and click the "search domain" button:

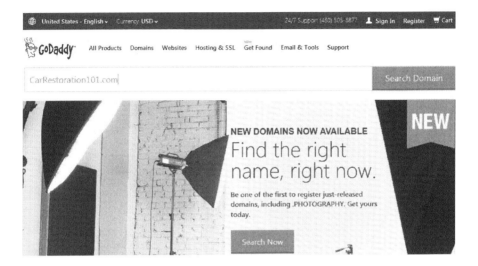

You'll then be taken to a page that tells you whether the domain name is available, which looks like this:

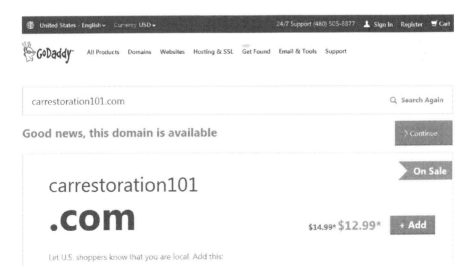

Or if it's not available then you'll see this:

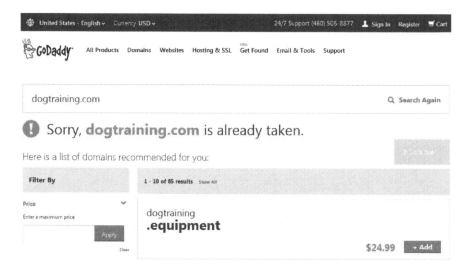

You'll note that if it's not available, you have the option of searching for another name or buying similar names (usually at a premium price). Go ahead and search for the next name on your list until you find one that's available.

Once you find one that's available, click the "+Add" next to the domain name to add it to your shopping cart. Then click the green "Continue" button to begin the checkout process:

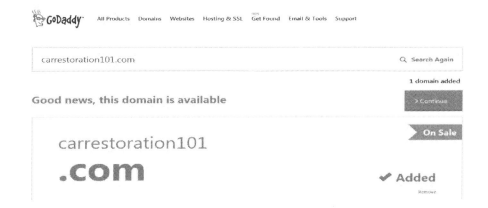

You'll be taken to a screen that looks like this:

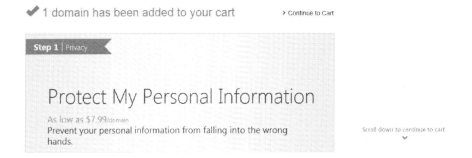

Let's go through these options:

- **Privacy.** If you leave your registration open to the public, then anyone can check the "who is" information on your website to find out your name, telephone number, address and email address. If you'd rather not make this information public, then you can choose to add a "privacy" option for a free, which will hide your information.

- **Website builder and hosting.** You do not need these, because you'll host through

<u>HostGator.com</u>, and I'll show you a free tool you can use to set up your site.

- **Email.** You do not need this option, because you'll automatically get unlimited email accounts once you set up your webhosting account.

Once you get through these options, click the orange "Continue to Cart" button at the bottom of the page. You'll be taken to the next step of the order process:

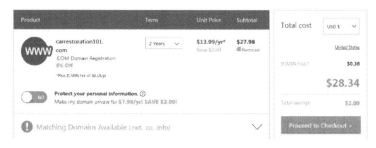

At this point you can choose whether to register your domain name for two years (which is the default setting), or one, three, five or ten years. Your choice. Select your option and click the orange "Proceed to Checkout" button. I typically purchase my domains one year at a time.

Now you'll either log into your existing account, or click the orange New Customer "Continue" button.

From there, fill out the order form to create your account and purchase your domain name.

Once you've completed your purchase, GoDaddy.com will send a confirmation email. Be sure to hang onto this, as you'll need it at tax time. Also, GoDaddy.com's welcome email will contain information about your account – be sure to write down your login information in a safe place.

> Note: You'll need to change your domain name servers (DNS) so that people arrive at your website when they enter your domain name into a browser or click on your links. However, you can't do this step until you set up your webhosting. So, let's make a decision about web site hosting…

2) <u>ESTABLISH</u> web site hosting. Think of web site hosting as your "place" on the internet. Every web site is hosted on a "server" which is – in the simplest of terms – a gigantic hard drive similar to your computer's hard drive. That's probably oversimplifying it a bit, but it's a comparison most people can understand.

You want to look for a hosting company that offers the following list of features…

- ✓ Ample disk space.
- ✓ Ample bandwidth (data transfer).
- ✓ Ability to password protect directories.
- ✓ Acceptable "uptime".
- ✓ Great customer service.
- ✓ Web-based file manager.

- ✓ An easy-to-use control panel.
- ✓ Unlimited email accounts and aliases.
- ✓ Advanced features that you may use later: MySQL databases, CGI-bin, SPAM blockers, Multiple domains, stats tracking, etc.

Now, there are literally **hundreds**, maybe even **thousands**, of hosting companies out there who will sell you web space to "*host*" your site for you. If you go to Google.com and search for "web site hosting", you'll find waaaaaay too many options to consider.

So, what I want to do is give you my <u>personal recommendation</u>. Please bear in mind that I am **NOT** using an affiliate link for this suggestion. I **DO NOT** get paid if you choose to use it. I simply recommend it on its own merits. I've personally used this host and have found it to be a first rate choice for hosting.

What is the host? <u>HostGator.com</u>.

This is a great host for the following reasons:

> 1. Good customer support. Not only can do you get access to plenty of videos and support documentation, but they have good customer service. Even if you're not very technically minded, their support is so thorough that you won't have any problems. I have found calling them, or clicking chat, has been the most efficient way to get support with Host Gator.

> 2. Good features. All of the HostGator.com shared-hosting options have all the features you need as described above—disk space, bandwidth, control panel and so on. I suggest

you choose the "Baby Plan," which allows you to add unlimited domains to your account. (Meaning you can set up multiple websites under that account without paying any additional fees.)

As mentioned, I suggest you choose the "Baby Plan," which is less than $10 a month (and if you talk to your accountant, you'll find it's likely a tax-deductible business expense, depending on where you live and what the tax laws are there). It's very inexpensive, yet it's a top-quality choice for running your business.

Nonetheless, sometimes people ask me about free hosting. Yes, free hosting is available, but I wouldn't recommend it. Here's why...

A word of warning: Now, I do want to quickly give you a word of warning – resist the temptation to use "free hosting" sites. The compromises you have to make with these free hosting sites just aren't worth it. Generally, they are slower, have poorer support and require you to place third party advertisements on your web site pages. Bottom line: You get what you pay for, or what you don't pay for.

Now, after you order a hosting package with HostGator, you'll be instructed on "domain nameservers" (AKA DNS).

> Note: Without going into too much technical explanation, a "nameserver" simply points the domain name to the hosted web space so people can actually visit your site. That's a good thing. ☺

To illustrate this, type your domain name into the address bar of your favorite browser and click ENTER.

What happens?

You either arrive at a page that informs you the page you're looking for is not available or you arrive at a page that informs you the page you're looking for is parked on behalf of your registrar. That's because, while you have a domain name, it isn't connected to any hosted web space at this point.

Once you change your domain name servers to point to HostGator, then your domain name (e.g., yourdomain.com) will point to your website – meaning people will be able to see whatever you upload to your site.

We'll get to that in just a bit.

Generally, a nameserver, as far as what's given to you, will look something like this...

```
ns1.hostingoption.com
ns2.hostingoption.com
```

Important: *The above are examples ONLY, and are NOT your actual domain name servers.*

You should have received a "welcome email" from HostGator.com when you purchased your hosting plan. Your two domain nameservers will be listed in that welcome email. If you cannot find this information, such as if you didn't receive this email, then contact HostGator.com's support and ask them what domain name servers you should use.

Once you have this information, then it's a matter of going back to GoDaddy.com to change this information.

Here's how... (please see the next page.)

Tutorial: How to Change Your Domain Nameservers (DNS)

Step 1. Go to www.godaddy.com and sign into your account.

You'll be taken to a screen that looks like this:

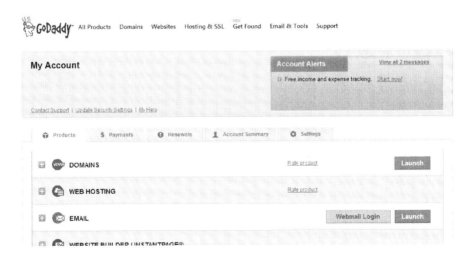

Step 2: Click on "Domains"

You'll be taken to a screen that looks like this, which will list your domains:

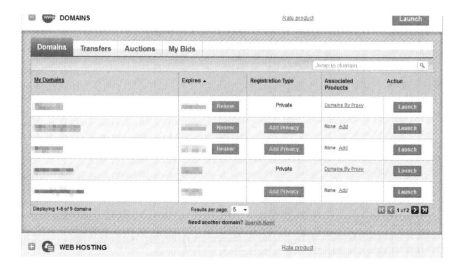

Step 3: Click on "launch" next to the domain name whose domain name servers you need to change.

You'll then see a screen like this, which will list information about that specific domain, along with options to manage this domain:

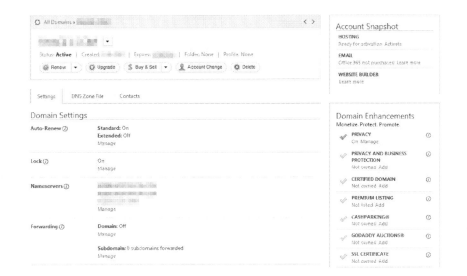

Take note that one of the options below "Domain Settings" is name servers.

Step 4: Click the "Manage" link listed below your existing nameservers.

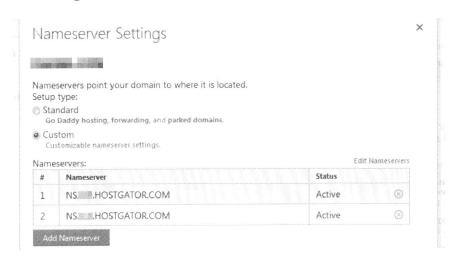

Step 5: Click "Edit Nameservers"

You'll get a screen that looks like this:

Step 6: Edit the nameservers. This is where you enter the nameservers as given to you in your HostGator welcome email. You'll need to enter both nameservers as provided to you.

Step 7: Click "OK" to save your two new nameservers.

And you're done! Congratulations! ☺

One note...

What needs to happen next is your domain name servers need to "propagate" around the world, which can take anywhere from a few hours to three days.

This means that even if you enter your domain name into your browser, your website may not show up immediately. It also means that it may show up intermittently – you'll see it, and then a few minutes later you can't access it any more. What's more, you may see it, but a friend may not be able to see it... or vice versa.

Just be patient. Within a few days, your domain should be fully propagated, and you as well as all your other visitors should be able to see your website when you go to your domain. (Assuming you have content on your website, which we'll get to in just a minute.)

So, now that we've gotten this far, it's time to begin looking at your order-processing options...

3) THINK about the order-process. You need some way to accept credit card and check payments online without you having to personally be involved in the transaction. This process needs to be instantaneous and efficient.

Again, as with most technology, there are **many different options** for your service provider. Vendors from all over the world are competing to get your business because they make money from you and the orders you process. They get a small percentage of **every sale** you make through their processing service.

This can make it **difficult** to select a third-party processor for beginners. Fortunately, I've been around the block more times than I care to remember, so I can certainly steer you in the right direction. Again, I don't make any money through these endorsements.

So here's the first resource I recommend: PayPal.

The reason I recommend them is because they have ZERO startup costs. If you are on a tight budget, they are a nice option because they don't require a setup fee to begin using their order processing service. Their fee-per-transaction is among the lowest available, as well. Payment for the orders you generate is automatically deposited into your PayPal account.

From there, you can choose to spend the money on a MasterCard debit card, get the money direct-deposited to your checking account or have a check mailed to you anytime you choose.

You can sell digital products AND physical products with their service, as well as recurring billing services such as membership sites. There are some drawbacks with poor customer service and an itchy trigger finger when it comes to freezing accounts for violations of their TOS, but still they are a very popular service that gets my recommendation.

If you don't already have an account, you can get one by going to
http://www.Paypal.com

In just a moment I'll show you how to quickly and easily create a payment button through PayPal. But first...

Need additional options? Check out these other recommended resources:

> Resource #2: Clickbank. I've been using Clickbank for several years. They are probably the easiest third-party

processor to get started with. There's a small one-time fee ($49 at the time of this writing) to get your account setup as well as a per transaction fee that's just a bit too high in my opinion. You can ONLY sell digital products and services with Clickbank. There are some steps you must complete to have your account activated. It's all very straightforward and explained thoroughly in their documentation. You get paid for your orders twice per month on or about the 1st and 15th of each month. With their built-in affiliate database system, this is another of my favorite resources: **http://www.Clickbank.com**

Resource #3: 2Checkout. I've heard from people using these guys for several of their products and have found them to offer a first-rate service as well. There is a one-time $49 fee to setup an account and your account is "live" in a matter of minutes. You can sell digital and physical products, and they also have a recurring billing feature for membership sites. You get paid via direct deposit to your checking account once per week. I've heard people have been very pleased with their service and don't hesitate in recommending them. **http://www.2Checkout.com**

So, those are some quality options you have to choose from in selecting who you will use to process your orders.

Note: Just in the interest of full disclosure, you CAN get your own merchant account, get your own gateway and process orders yourself, but that's not something I recommend that you do at this point. Having your own merchant account, etc. is not beneficial to most people until after they are producing a high volume of orders.

For now, it's best for you to choose from one of these three quality vendors.

Obtaining an order link and setting up your special report for the actual order approval and confirmation process **will vary depending upon which vendor you choose**. However, since PayPal requires no upfront fee and it's easy to use, I'm going to provide a PayPal tutorial for you...

Tutorial: How to Create a Payment Button Through PayPal

Step 1: Log into your account at PayPal.com

I'm going to assume that you already have a PayPal.com account, as most people do. If you don't yet have one, then obviously your first step to sign up here.

You'll need to have your bank account and other information at your fingertips, and it may take a few days to completely set up your account (as PayPal will verify your bank account by making a small deposit in it).

Once it's all set up, however, you can log in and move onto step 2.

Note: Usually there is an advertisement right after you log in. Skip this by clicking the "Proceed to Account Overview" button.

Step 2: Click on the "Merchant Services" button on the top navigation bar.

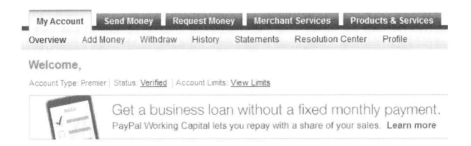

Step 3: Click on "Create Payment Buttons for Your Website

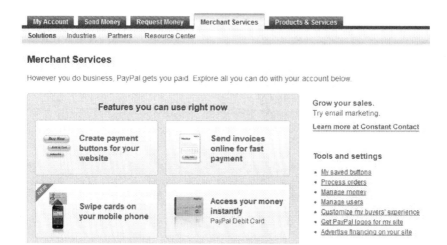

Step 4: Click on "Create a Button"

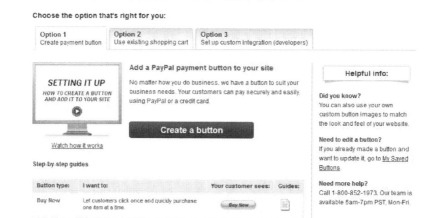

You'll see this screen next:

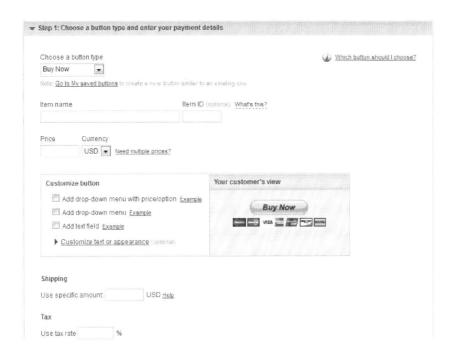

Step 5: Fill out the requested information for PayPal's "Step 1"

PayPal's Step 1 for creating a "buy now" button includes the following options:

- *Choose a button type*: choose the Buy Now option.
- *Item Name*: Enter a name that describes the report, such as "Dog Training 101 Report."
- *Item ID*: This is a number that you assign for your own personal records. Using the dog training example, you might assign a number like DT001 (for dog training report #001).
- *Price*: Enter your price and choose your currency. (E.G., 7.00 USD)
- *Customize Button*: You can skip these options.

- *Shipping*: Leave this blank.
- *Tax*: Talk to your accountant about this option (whether you need to collect sales tax).
- *Merchant Account IDs*. Choose the "use my primary email address" option, and then choose which email you'd like to use (if you have more than one email assigned to your PP account).

Once you get through these options, then...

Step 6: Skip the "Step 2" link.

If you click on Step 2, you would see these options:

However, these are advanced options that you can skip.

So, unless you are tracking profits and losses using PayPal, you can leave all of these options in their default state and move on to the next step.

Step 7: Click on the "Step 3" option.

You'll see this screen:

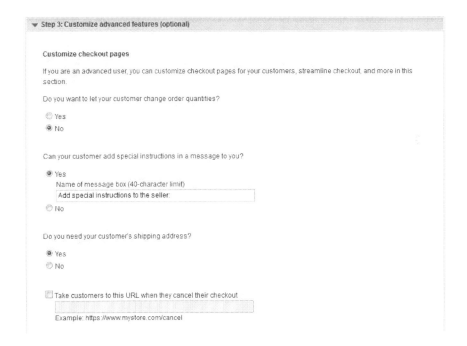

These too are advanced options, which you will want to complete (especially where it asks you about entering links):

- Do you want to let the customer change quantity options? Either option is fine. You can choose "yes" if you think your customers might opt to purchase a copy for a friend at the same time. (It's fairly unlikely this would happen, however.)

- Can your customer add special instructions? You can choose "yes" for this option. Again, it's unlikely your customer will add any instructions, but it's always good to give your customer a chance to leave you a note. Just be sure that you check all orders for "special instructions" if you do choose yes for this option.
- Do you need your customer's shipping address? The default is "yes," but since this a downloadable product you can change this to "no."
- Take customers to this URL when they cancel their checkout. Generally, you'll want this to point to your sales letter, which is generally the home page of your website (e.g., www.yourdomain.com).
- Take customers to this URL when they finish their checkout. This is the URL (link) of your download page. In other words, when people finish checking out at PayPal, they'll be taken to a page where you thank them for their order and give them a link to download their report. I'll give you an example and show you how to create this page just a little bit later in this guide.
- Advanced variables. Unless you are an advanced user, you can skip this option.

Once you complete these options, then look to the bottom of your page...

Step 8: Click the orange "Create Button"

You'll come to this page, which will have the code for you payment button:

Step 9: Click the "select code" button to highlight the button code.

Step 10: Hover over this code and right click your mouse. Choose "copy."

Step 11: Paste this code into your website (or into a text document for now).

You do this by hovering over the place in your sales letter (the HTML source file) or other document where you want the code to appear, right clicking your mouse, and choosing "paste." Then be sure to save your file and, if it's the HTML page, upload it to your website.

I'll talk about how to do all of this tech stuff in a little more detail just a bit later. For now, if you don't have a web page, then save your button code into a text file for easy retrieval later.

That's it – that's all you have to do to create a payment button at PayPal.

If you're using any other payment processor, then the process is much the same. You log into the payment processor, use their control panel to create the button, and then copy and paste the button code into your sales letter where you want the payment button to appear.

From that point, there are a few minor things to do in finalizing your order process.

Create your <u>SALES</u> page. This is the primary page at your web site that will consist of your mini-sales letter that we spoke at length about in our last session.

Where it reads "Click Here" to order (or whatever you chose in writing your mini-sales letter) have that linked to the order URL provided to you by PayPal (or the third-party vendor you chose).

Again, you can hire someone to setup the technical aspects of this for you should you choose not to do it yourself. However, here's a tutorial you can use to set it up yourself...

Tutorial: How to Create an HTML Sales Letter

Step 1: Install an .html editor.

I suggest you use the Coffee Cup editor, which is available for Windows: http://www.coffeecup.com/free-editor/ or for Mac: http://www.coffeecup.com/osx/web-editor/.

Click the download link to download the executable file to your computer. Once it has downloaded, then click on the file on your computer and follow the prompts to install the software on your computer.

Step 2: Select a sales letter template.

If you don't know anything about creating an .html page, then this project will be easiest for you if you start with a sales letter template. You can run a search for "html sales letter template" in Google, which will give you both free and paid options.

For simplicity's sake, here's a link to a package of 20 basic .html sales letter templates available for free: http://infosteals.com/templates/20-free-css-html-sales-letter-templates (I'll use Template #12 for this tutorial. You can follow using this same template or the template of your choice.)

Step 3: Open your sales letter template in Coffee Cup.

To do this, open up Coffee Cup on your computer. You'll see this screen:

Click on "Open Existing Files," and then navigate to the place on your computer where you've stored your chosen website template. Once you've found it, click on it to open it in the Coffee Cup editor. (Note: Your .html file will be called index.html or index.htm.)

Step 4: Create a "split view" screen.

When you first open up your index.html file, you're going to see all the html code—which probably looks like a lot of gobbled-gook. Coffee Cup is a WYSIWYG (what you see is what you get) editor, meaning as you work within the code you'll be able to see what the file will look like.

To achieve this, you need to go to split screen. You do this clicking on "View" and then choosing "split screen preview" as shown below:

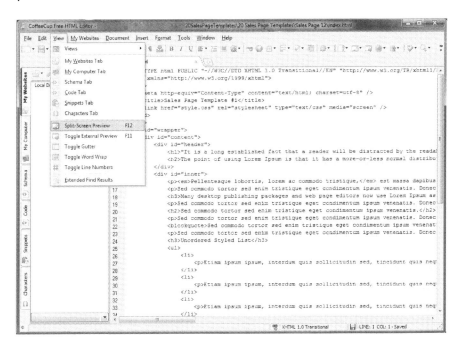

You can then adjust these two windows in any way you like, such as making the preview screen bigger

Step 5: Edit the sales letter template.

Now it's time for you to actually edit the template. You can do this by highlighting a portion of the preview pane that you want to work with, which will automatically highlight the code. In most cases, all you have to do is click on the section you'd like to highlight, such as the headline, a specific paragraph, etc, and the software will highlight the entire section in the code for you.

For example, click on the headline of the sales letter template, and the software will automatically highlight the entire line of text in the code, as shown:

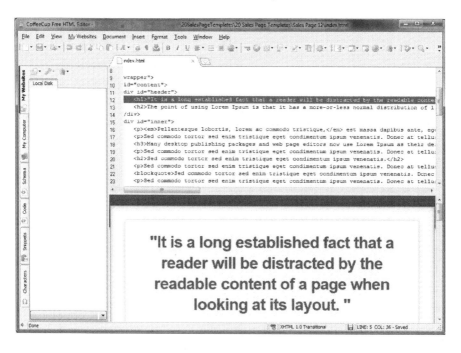

Now, what you'll see in this example is a line that looks like this:

```
<h1>"It is a long established fact that a
reader will be distracted by the readable
content of a page when looking at its layout.
"</h1>
```

The <h1> code is a tag that tells browsers to create a big headline. Everything between the <h1> opening tag and its closing tag (</h1>) can be edited to change the headline on your sales letter. So, delete the line that starts with "it is a long established fact…"

And replace it with your own sales letter headline. Be sure to leave the quotation marks intact, as sales letter headlines should be in quotes.

You can use this same process throughout the entire template to replace the existing "placeholder" text with text from your actual sales letter. Simply click on the section you want to change, and edit the actual text from the sales letter.

Note: Unless you understand HTML, do NOT edit any of the HTML codes, which are generally found between these brackets: < and >. (For example, the code for bolding is , and the code to stop bolding text is . Don't modify these codes. If you do accidentally modify or delete something, then click on the horseshoe shaped "undo" icon at the top of Coffee Cup, of click "ctrl+z" if you're using Windows.

If you want to format the actual look of the text on the page, then highlight the text you'd like to format, and click on "Format" from the navigation menu as shown:

You'll see plenty of options appear in the drop down menu under "Format."

From there you can choose to bold, italicize, underline or even change the color or size of the text. Simply click on the option you want, and it will change your highlighted text to your preferred format.

Note: Be sure to retrieve the PayPal button code that you created earlier and copy and paste it into your HTML code file where you want it to appear. For example, on the template I've been using for this tutorial, you might paste the

code right at the very bottom of the
sales letter. Simply take out the part
that says "Thank you for using this sales
page CSS/HTML template" and replace that
text with the PayPal button code.

Be sure to save any changes you make (you should
save the file as index.html).

The above "quick and dirty" tutorial basically gives
you everything you need to know to replace the text
in a template and format the text to alter the look of
it. If you need to do something more advanced or if
you run into problems, you can use Coffee Cup's
tutorials, documentation and other support.

Here's their "getting started" guide:
http://www.coffeecup.com/help/articles/html-editor-
quick-start-guide/

Here's their knowledge base of articles:
http://www.coffeecup.com/help/articles/search?tag=H
TML+Editor

And here are their community support forums where
you can ask questions about the HTML editor:
http://www.coffeecup.com/forums/html-editor/

Once you create your sales page and save it as
index.html, then you can create your fulfillment page:

Create your FULFILLMENT page. The other
accompanying HTML page you need to have created is
your "fulfillment" page. This is the page at your site
that your customers will be directed to after they have
finished paying for your special report. This page

should include complete instructions on how to obtain the special report they've ordered. In our tutorial, this will include a "download link" that the customer can click on to immediately download your special report onto their computer.

I've included a simple template download/thank you page that you can use to create your own page. You've already learned how to do all of these steps just a bit earlier in this guide, so this tutorial is just a quick refresher of how to modify the file and upload the file...

Tutorial: Modifying Included Download Page Template

Step 1: Open your HTML editor.

This is the "Coffee Cup" software or your chosen HTML editor. Choose "open existing files" and then navigate to the place on your computer where you saved the download page template that was included with this course.

Step 2: Click on "View" and choose "Split Screen Preview" from the upper navigation menu.

This lets you view the code as well a preview of how your download page will appear on your website.

Step 3: Highlight the first part that needs to be changed.

You'll want to highlight the words within the top panel, which is where the actual code is located. These are the words that begin with: "[insert the download link here...

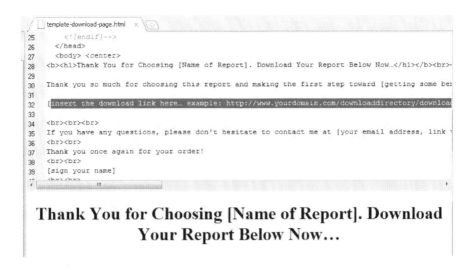

Go ahead and delete that entire line, including the brackets []. Leave your mouse in place, because you're going to replace that text...

Step 4: Type in your download link as shown.

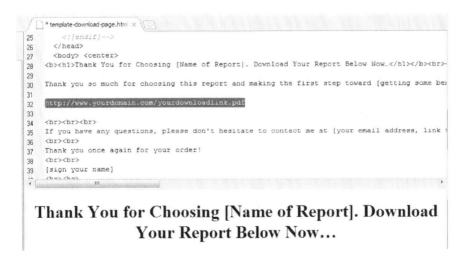

> Note: Creating a download link is a relatively easy process. It includes marrying your domain name URL with the file name of your special report. Let's

```
look at an example -

* If your domain URL is
http://www.SmallReportsFortuneMadeEasy.co
m and
* If your file name is
srfortunemadeeasy.pdf, then your
"download link" would be…

http://www.SmallReportsFortune.com/srfort
unemadeeasy.pdf

Please note the / between your domain
name and the file name.
Please also note that the "download link"
won't actually work until you upload your
files to your site.
```

Tip: The file name of your sales page should be "index.html" and the title of your fulfillment page should be something like "ty_dload.html."

However, that isn't a particularly protected download page. You can make it more protected by making a download page name that's hard to guess, such as "ty_dload_832832.html" (that's just an example).

You could protect this page in other ways, such as by creating password protected directories. However, I'm not going to go over this more advanced instruction, simply because they aren't necessary for you to get started this early in your business. I'd recommend that you learn about these processes after you've established your first order.

Step 5: Make your download link clickable.

You'll notice that merely typing the download link into the document doesn't make the link clickable, so that's what we need to do next.

First, be sure the link is highlighted code as shown in the previous screenshot (in this example, the link is http://www.yourdomain.com/yourdownloadlink.pdf).

Next, click on "Insert" from the top navigation menu and choose "Link" from the dropdown list of options as shown:

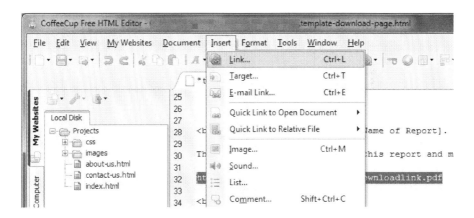

Now you need to type or copy in your actual download link into the "URL to Link To" section:

Note that for this example I typed in: "http://www.yourdomain.com/yourdownloadlink.pdf" as the "link to" URL. However, you need to type in your actual domain name and actual .pdf file name.

Click "OK" once you've entered in the link to your .pdf.

Then verify your link clickable – it should be blue in the bottom preview pane as shown below:

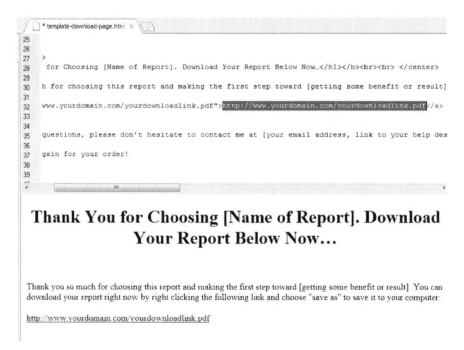

Step 6: Make the other required changes.

Now you simply rinse and repeat – use the same instructions as above to change the other information in the template. Highlight the text you want to change in the upper panel (code) section, delete it, and replace it as described above.

Step 7: Save your download page.

Once you've made all your changes, then click "File" on the upper left side of your screen and choose "save as." Do two things:

> 1. Save it with the rest of your web files so they're all in one easy-to-find place.

> 2. Rename the download page to your preferred name (take note it must end with .html).

> > Note: Whatever you name this file is the filename you'll use when you create your PayPal button.
> >
> > Let's say you call this file "ty1721.html," and you upload it to the main directory of your website. When you create your PayPal payment button, the link you'd direct people to after they completed payment would be http://www.yourdomain.com/ty1721.html (where you'd replace "yourdomain.com" with your actual domain name).

That's all there is to modifying these files and preparing them for upload. So now let's move onto that step...

4) UPLOAD your files.   "Uploading" is the process by which you transfer files from your computer to your web site. Generally speaking, you have two options for "uploading" your files...

Option #1: **Software**. There are several "FTP" software programs available that you can purchase which will be useful to your long-term business. Here is one that our team has used "WS_FTP" (available in "Home" and "Professional" versions) which can be purchased at http://www.Ipswitch.com. It comes complete with instructions on using and is a great tool to have. If you have the fifty or so bucks within your budget to invest in it, this is your best option.

(Note: There are many other transfer software programs available that you can find by searching Google.com or Download.com. However, this is the only one that I have used, so it's the only one I can recommend.)

Option #2: **Server**. The other option is to use the file transfer function available through your hosting company. Every quality hosting service will offer this feature. I've provided a tutorial below for how to upload files using your HostGator.com control panel.

With either of these options, make sure you "upload" the files to your MAIN directory at the site in order for the links to work properly as I've described. This is also known as your "root" folder or "public" folder or "WWW" folder.

The files that you'll want to upload are...

✓ Sales page.
✓ Fulfillment page.
✓ Special report.

✓ Applicable site graphics.

Here's how...

Tutorial: Uploading Your Sales Page to Your Website

If you purchased your webhosting through HostGator, then you'll have access to a control panel that includes a file manager – this is the place where you can upload files, delete files and generally manage your website. Here's how to upload your sales page (which is your index.html page)...

Step 1: Log into your control panel.

When you first signed up to HostGator, you should have received a link and login instructions for your control panel – please check your welcome email for more information. However, generally you can log in by going to www.yourdomain.com/cpanel (replacing "yourdomain.com" with your actual domain name).

Step 2: Scroll down to the "Files" section and click on "File Manager"

Step 3: Double click on the "public_html" icon on the right side of your screen.

Note that, it's NOT the "public_ftp" folder, you should double click on the "public_html" folder icon.

Step 4: Double click on the folder next to the name of your website on the right side of your screen.

You are now in the main directory of your website. This is where you will upload the index.html page, which will show as the front page of your website. So let's do that...

Step 5: Click on "upload" on the navigation bar near the top of your screen.

This will open a new window.

Step 6: Click "Browse."

Now you need to navigate to the place on your computer where you saved your index.html file (which is your sales letter). On the next page is an example of what it looks like on my computer where I used the sales page template to create my page:

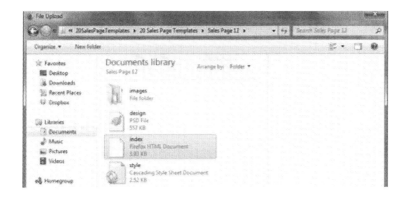

Step 7: Upload the index.html file

You do this by clicking on the selected file and choosing "open." You will be taken back to this screen...

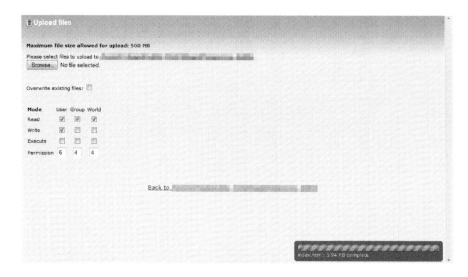

... take note that at the bottom of the screen there is confirmation that the upload was a success.

Step 8: Upload other files

If you used the sales page template which came with images, then you'll need to navigate to your "image" folder and upload the template's images. You do this by:

- Click the link that looks similar to: "back to home/username/public_html/domain" – this will take you back to the main file manager page.
- Confirm that you are in the main directory of your website.

- You should see a folder called "images." Double click on it.
- Now click "upload" and use the instructions above to upload your sales page template images into your existing image folder on your website.

That's all there is to it. You can use these same instructions whenever you need to upload files to your site, delete files, etc.

Is Your Site Live?

As soon as you upload your index.html sales page, the world will be able to see your website (assuming your domain name has propagated around the world). In other words, your site will be live.

If you're not yet ready to make your site go live, then you can do one of two things:

- **Don't upload your index.html page.** People who visit your site will see a page with your site's folders listed (like the CGI folder and image folder). It's clear the site isn't ready, but this isn't particularly professional. As such, I suggest the following…

- **Upload a "Coming Soon" page.** You do this by creating a page called index.html that simply says "coming soon" or whatever else you want it to say, and then uploading it as described above. Just be sure you save it somewhere special on your computer so that you do not confuse it with your sales page which has the same file name – you don't want to accidentally write over your sales page.

- Once your sales page is ready, then upload it as described above. You'll be asked if you want to overwrite the existing "coming soon" index.html page. Click yes to overwrite, and your website will then go live.

That's how you upload the sales page. Now your final step is to upload the download page AND your .pdf file to your website. You use the exact same procedure here as described above for uploading these files to your website. Refer to the above tutorial for specifics and screenshots, but here's the overview:

1. Log into your control panel (typically yourdomain.com/cpanel)

2. Scroll down to "Files" and choose "File Manager"

3. Double click on "public_html" and double click on your website to go into its root directory.

4. Click on "Upload."

5. Browse for your download page on your computer hard drive, click on it, and choose "open" when you find it.

6. Confirm on the next page that the file uploaded.

7. Browse for and upload your report (the file ending in .pdf).

8. Navigate to your actual download page on your website (e.g., yourdomain.com/your-download-page-name.html) to confirm that it's online. Click on the download link to verify that you can download the .pdf report.

That's all there is to it! Personally, I find it easier to hire a web developer to do the above tasks. I recently completed a project to have three pages completed and it cost me just over 100 bucks. Well worth it to me! You can find freelancers online at a site like upwork.com or even fiverr.com. Just be careful who you choose to work with as they will have access to your account information and logins.

When you have your files "uploaded" to your site, it's time for the final step...

5) <u>PREPARE</u> for your first order. That is, you "*test*" the entire process from start to finish in order to make certain everything is working properly.

Specifically, here is a quick checklist of things you'll want to do in order to verify the order process...

o Type your domain name into the address bar in your internet browser and click the ENTER button to visit the site.

o Upon arriving at your web site, verify that the page loads properly, with all images and text formatted in the desired layout.

o Click on your "order link" as if you were placing an order and verify that it transfers you to an order page with your third-party vendor.

o Verify that the information contained on the order page is correct, specifically the name of the product being ordered and the price for that product.

o Either place a real order or mock order to verify proper processing and delivery. If you choose, go ahead and complete the information needed to actually order the product. If you'd rather not, then type the fulfillment page "URL" (For example: http://www.YourDomainNameHere.com/ty_dloa d.html).

o Verify that the fulfillment page loads properly with images and text formatted in the desired layout.

o Click on your download link and attempt to download the special report file to your computer.

o Open the special report file that you've just downloaded and make sure it is the correct version of your report and everything looks as planned.

If everything checks out properly, then "congratulations", you're ready to take orders!

If something doesn't check out properly, don't panic. Just look for what went wrong, make some corrections and try it again.

Now, after you've setup your site to sell the special report as I've described here, it's simply a matter of getting visitors to your site to view what you have to offer.

That process begins with sending an email to your existing list and extends to trying a variety of advertising, promotion and marketing techniques. Obviously, this is beyond the scope of our course here, but I do want to mention a great resource to help you in generating "traffic" (I.E. visitors) to your web site...

- ❖ http://www.PartnerTrafficMadeEasy.com -- great 20-page tutorial there.

Now, having gotten this far, I want to take you through one final session where I'm going to explain something that has never been revealed before: a systematic approach for getting from one special report all the way to a six-figure business...

How To Turn Small Reports Into A Six-Figure Business

We've covered a <u>LOT</u> of ground thus far, haven't we?! I'm excited about the possibilities here for you. I know this works. I have seen many profit from this business model for over 10 years.

That's a long time in internet years ... the web literally changes overnight. So, when something like this plan stands the test of **internet time**, it's a keeper.

But, it's not enough to know everything that I've taught you so far. That's a great start, but that, in itself, will not develop a *"six-figure income"* from small reports.

We know all about the *"small reports"*, now it's time to talk about the *"small fortune"*!

The 6 Phases Of A Six-Figure Small Report Business

After analyzing, tweaking, and improving the process, we've been able to establish a unique set of "phases" that will allow you to take your *"small reports"* business to the $100,000 / year level and beyond.

I've <u>never</u> made this 6-phase plan available publicly.

Until now. ☺

You're getting a ***first look*** at a very unique business model in that it's relatively easy-to-do, while possessing the potential to be a **very lucrative** revenue generator for anyone who makes it to phase #6.

What I want to do now is take you through each of the **six phases** of the "*Small Reports Fortune Made Easy*" plan.

> **Note:** As a sidebar before we begin, let me stress that during all that I am about to explain to you, it's important that you continue creating ONE new special report each month for the next 12 months (and beyond, if you choose!). If you have any troubles developing this content, or if you're just looking for a way to create it more quickly, then I suggest you check out my content templates and resource package at www.contentwritingmadeeasy.com.

So, with that foundation laid, let's take a look at the "*6 phases*" of a small reports six-figure business...

Phase #1
Write Your Initial Small Report And Promote It

Confucius said, "*a journey of a thousand miles begins with a single step*". (Or something like that.)

I say, "*a journey of a six-figure income begins with a single small report*".

Aaah, two great philosophers. Ain't it grand! ☺

Seriously, don't think your first small report to be insignificant. It's anything but insignificant. It's a critical first step towards establishing a hefty annual income.

So, phase one begins with an appropriate step: write your initial report and promote it. That is, walk through the process that we've explored thus far in this course.

- ✓ Get that first small report ready to sell.
- ✓ Write your mini-sales letter.
- ✓ S.E.T.U.P. your site.

And then start promoting it so you can see orders.

Now, I can't give you a crash course in promotion. That's not what this presentation is all about. But, I will give you four quick things to do in order to drive visitors (Aka "traffic") to your web site in order to begin seeing orders.

1. **Mention Your Small Report To Your Contacts**. Begin with those with whom you already have a relationship. If you have an email list (I.E. Newsletter, mini-course, customer, etc.) then the first order of business is to announce your small report to it. Setup a signature file for all of your outgoing emails – you might as well promote your small report when you answer your emails! If you are involved in a "community" (I.E. Chat rooms, message boards, membership sites, mastermind group, club, Facebook groups, etc.) then mention your small report, as appropriate. Promote your small report to those you know

first. And, if you don't already have a list of some type, you need to begin building one. I suggest you use my traffic system at www.partnertrafficmadeeasy.com to learn how to grow your business.

2. **Write And Distribute An Article**. Everyone knows that writing 500-700 word articles that you allow others to publish to their own lists and at their sites, blogs, etc., is a great way to generate free publicity for your site through your attached "resource box" at the close of your article. One of the first things you should do to promote your small report is write a short article that is RELATED to the topic of your small report. In your resource box for the ezine article, announce your small report. Send this ezine article to your existing contacts (I.E. everything we just talked about in #1), send it directly to bloggers who publish guest articles, AND submit it for publication at the popular ezine article directories, etc. I personally recommend that you use a service such as http://www.iSnare.com to handle these submissions for you as they can be quite time-consuming.

3. **Post Messages At Appropriate Message Boards**. Almost every major marketplace has numerous high-traffic forums (Aka "message boards") where you can ask and answer questions related to the topic. In each of these "posts" that you make, you can oftentimes include a "resource link" to promote whatever you want. (Check the posting terms at your favorite forum before proceeding). So, get

involved. Answer questions, join discussions, ask for advice, etc. – and include a one sentence link to your small report web site as it pertains to the post you're making.

Example #1: let's suppose someone has asked a question at your favorite homeschooling hang-out such as, "The lessons seem to be taking too much time, how can I speed things up?" You would post a helpful reply and then insert a resource link for your small report such as, "Click Here for 17 Ways To Save Time Without Sacrificing Quality". Just like that, you're off and running.

Example #2: Let's suppose someone else has asked a question at this same homeschooling forum such as, "What are some great ideas for 'field trips' that you've used with your children?" You would post a helpful reply and then insert a resource link for your small report such as, "Click Here for 17 Ways To Free Up Time For More Fun Field Trips".

Example #3: Let's suppose a third person has asked a question at this forum such as, "What's the best curriculum to use when starting out for the first time?" You would post a helpful reply and then insert a resource link for your small report such as, "Click Here for 17 Ways

Beginning Homeschoolers Can Save Time".

Do you see how this works? Always bring the conversation to YOUR small report. Make it applicable to whatever is being discussed in the post.

4. Dedicate Time To Learning One New Marketing Method Each Week.

There are many, many, many different ways to drive traffic to your small report web site. I would recommend that you spend a couple hours every week learning about how to promote your web site. Be careful not to get overwhelmed – and resist the temptation to go and buy every course out there that seems to be exactly what you're looking for. Set a budget for what you want to spend on your "education" and stick to it.

You can find helpful information on these subjects by searching at http://www.Google.com for phrases such as...

- "How to build a list"
- "How to write an ezine article"
- "How to promote on forums"
- "How to use AdWords®"
- "How to promote my site"
- "How to generate web site traffic"
-

I also strongly recommend that you check out my "Free to Fee Made Easy" system, which will teach you how to create "free samples" to convert browsers into buyers. Check it out here: http://freetofeesystemmadeeasy.com/

Note: While it is certainly not a "comprehensive tutorial", I've included my own checklist for promoting products at the close of this course. Consider it a free of charge "bonus" with my compliments. It will give you a good overview of what I do to promote my own products. You can use it as a basis for some of your own promotion. It will be especially helpful to you once you've arrived at phase #3.

So, that's "*phase #1*". Write and promote your initial small report. Then, on to the next phase...

Phase #2
Create 4-7 Related Small Reports And Cross-Promote Series

Quite obviously, ONE small report isn't going to make you a fortune. It's going to take a bit more to get into some "serious" income. So, let's take things up a level. In "phase #2", you create 4-7 related reports and then cross-promote the series.

There are a couple of "guidelines" that I want to make here as recommendations before I talk about cross promotion.

Guideline #1 –
Make sure the additional small reports are all "related" to each other.

In order for this to really work well for you, each of your small reports needs to be connected in some way so that when a customer buys one of them, they are automatically qualified to buy all of them because of their INTEREST in the subject matter of all of them. The classic example I use is "weight loss". Consider how one customer wanting to lose weight would have an interest in each of these related, but decidedly different, reports...

- A small report on losing 10 pounds.
- A small report on raising metabolism.
- A small report on ways to burn an extra 100 calories.
- A small report on low-calorie recipes.
- A small report on toning up flabby muscles.

Do you see how all of these are DIFFERENT, but they are also CONNECTED by their common bond? This dramatically raises the likelihood that your customer will make multiple purchases from this series ... perhaps even buying them all!

Guideline #2:
Create at least one new small report per month, preferably two.

How quickly you get to the more lucrative phases of your business is completely up to you. My recommendation is that you create at least one additional small report per month. For this phase, you need a minimum of four small reports, while phase #3 requires that you have at least six small reports completed. At a rate of one-per-month, this would take you four months to complete phase #2 and six months to complete phase #3. If you double your production to TWO small reports each month, you would reduce your time needed to complete these phases and really start to see significant progress.

One per month is fine. Two per month is optimal. Don't try for anything more or you'll be bombarding your contacts with TOO MUCH, not to mention you'd probably overtax yourself.

Now, as you create these additional small reports, I want you to do everything I mentioned in phase #1 for each of them. In addition, add the following "cross promotion" steps to complete phase #2...

✓ **Cross promote inside the reports themselves**. In each of your small reports include references to your other reports. You can do this in <u>three strategic, yet subtle ways</u>...

> 1) Include an "About The Author" page where you mention all of the small reports you've written, along with links to your sales pages for each.
>
> 2) Mention the existing reports in the actual text if and when it is relevant. In other words, if you're talking about something that you've explained thoroughly in an earlier report, reference

the report.

3) Create a "recommended resources" page to include at the end of your small report which has a brief description and web site link for all of your existing reports.

Every NEW report you create (you know, ONE per month) should have these cross promotion points included – and updated to showcase ALL of your offers.

✓ **Cross promote on the "fulfillment" pages**. Each of your small reports has a "fulfillment" page as we've talked about earlier. This is the web page where the customer downloads the small report that they've ordered from you. This is a great spot for you to mention all of your other related reports by simply listing "Other Small Reports by Your Name". If you offer a discount for additional purchases, you should see an increase your orders.

✓ **Cross promote by using "upsell" pages**. That is, you create an "upsell" page at your existing sales pages to offer additional reports.

The "normal" sales process that we've talked about works like this...

1. Visitor clicks on your order link and arrives at third-party processor.
2. Visitor places order and arrives at your "fulfillment" page.

The "upsell" sales process works like this...

    1. Visitor clicks on your order link and arrives at an "intermediate" page.

    2. Visitor has two choices of order links:

        - Order only the original small report.

        - Order a combination of two or more reports.

    3. Visitor makes their choice and places order.

    4. Visitor arrives at the APPROPRIATE "fulfillment" page.

In addition to the web pages that we've talked about in our earlier sections, you'd need to create an "intermediate order page" and an additional "fulfillment page" that has download links to the combination package being offered as the "upsell".

I don't have time to explain this concept any further. If you need help, you can do some research at Google.com, etc. I just want to mention this as a great way to cross promote your series of reports.

✓ **<u>Cross promote</u> in your follow-up emails**. You should always send emails to your customers "after the sale" thanking them for their order, etc. In these follow-up emails you can again make reference to your entire series of reports.

You can even provide the customers with your ezine articles sent out one per week that you've written to promote the small reports. This will give you regular contact with your customers, provide them with additional free content, and give you the continued opportunity to promote your series of small reports.

I can't stress enough how profitable this type of cross promotion system can be.
Not only are you SELLING each of these **new** small reports, but they automatically PROMOTE your **existing** reports to create an entire myriad of extra orders!

So, once you've completed this phase – and it should take from 2-6 months, depending upon how frequently you create new small reports – it's time to move on to phase #3 which is where your sales should take a significant jump...

Phase #3
**Bundle Several Small Reports
Into A Higher-Priced Package**

One of the drawbacks up until this point is that you'll primarily be doing all of your marketing yourself. That is, you won't find a lot of active affiliates and joint venture partners to promote your small reports simply because the amount of profit per sale isn't very good.

> In other words, if you sell a special report for $17 and pay 50% commission for sales referrals from affiliates and partners, that would only be about $8.00 per order. It would take a LOT of orders for the affiliate to earn any significant commissions from you.

And affiliates are **fickle**. They go where the money is.

If they can make $25, $50 or more per sale promoting something else, they'll certainly do that as opposed to promoting your small report in most cases.

So, here's where things **change** in that regard.

You'll now be able to ATTRACT affiliates and joint venture partners to get busy promoting your offers! Instead of one person (you!) doing all of the marketing, you can now enlist an entire sales army of people advertising your site.

Here's how -

Take 6-7 of your small reports and bundle them into one package that sells for a higher price.

If you've got 6 small reports that you've been selling for $20.00 each, that's $120.00 in value. Create a package that you offer for $77 or $97. That gives you something more lucrative for affiliates to promote and instantly gets you larger chunks of profit per transaction.

Instead of needing to sell 5,000 reports at $20.00 each to generate $100,000 per year, you only need to sell approximately 1,000 packages at $97.00 each to reach the same goal. That's significantly easier. Especially when you factor in the efforts of an active affiliate team.

Now, without trying to oversimplify things, there are a couple of steps you need to take in order to master this phase that I want to quickly mention...

1. **Setup a separate domain with a new sales letter**.

   This new package of yours needs to have its own domain name with its own sales letter. I strongly recommend that you don't simply say, *"Buy 6 of my reports for only a fraction of their total cost if sold separately."* That's a big, big mistake as far as the ability to convert visitors into paying customers.

   What you want to do is create a totally new concept for the compilation of your reports. Think of it as a one-time fee *"membership site"* where each of your small reports is part of an overall system of modules.

   Write your sales letter from the standpoint of no longer being an isolated small report, but now a complete "system".

   Let me give you the ultimate example of this: www.contentwritingmadeeasy.com

   Go ahead and click on that link, and you'll see I've created a huge package of templates and resources for people who use content to grow their business.

   I could easily sell each of these resources separately for $10 to $50 each. But since these templates and resources are all tightly related, I've compiled them into one package.

So, while some of these were all full-length products and not small reports, the point is the same. They can all be combined into one mega-package for a premium price. This is what I did to create a high-ticket, high-value package, and it's what you can do too.

So, you need a separate site, with a separate sales letter.

2. **Start an affiliate program and recruit partners**. The second thing you need to do is start an affiliate program and begin recruiting partners to promote your new package through their unique affiliate link.

   Affiliates will love 50% commission on a $77-$97 package.

   One of the reasons that I recommend that you use Clickbank.com to process your orders is because they <u>automatically</u> set you up with an affiliate program for your account. They track orders. They award commissions based on the percentage you want. They pay your affiliates. It's all handled by them which is what makes it an attractive option.

   You can research Google to learn more about how to land affiliates. You can also check out this page: http://www.partnertrafficmadeeasy.com/, which will give you some hints for making the most of your affiliates.

The important thing is that you bundle your existing RELATED reports into one package that you sell for a premium price and begin locating affiliate partners to advertise on your behalf.

Note: Be sure to provide your affiliates with each of those ezine articles you've written so they can publish them to their own lists and blogs, and encode your resource box with their affiliate link. This gives them quality content they can pass on to their contacts while simultaneously endorsing your package.

And with that, we begin talking about phase #4...

Phase #4
Develop A Comprehensive Promotion Outlet To Showcase Reports

By this time, you've got some assets that you need to showcase. It's time to develop your presence online as a force to be reckoned with! ☺

One of the progressive steps that you need to take in building your business is to develop a *"home"* that's all about you and what you offer. In other words, you need a portal web site that is the entry way to everything you have to sell.

It's important that you create this kind of base camp for a couple of reasons...

1. **People will begin to <u>REFERENCE</u> you**. As you become more and more prominent within your market, people will begin to talk about you (hopefully, in a good way! ☺). They'll reference things you've said in your small reports, articles, etc. They'll interview you. They'll point out things they've learned from you. They'll quote you. And so forth. You'll be identified with that site and people will begin to visit that site.

2. **People will begin to <u>RESPECT</u> you**. As you begin to win fans of your writing, you'll find that you'll gain a following. People will want more and more of you. If they find something about your writing helpful and informative, they'll seek out other things you've written. By having a portal site that showcases everything you offer, you'll give others the opportunity to purchase and assimilate as much of your materials as they choose. I very rarely find that a customer only orders ONE offer...most order many.

So, having this portal site is the next phase of business development for you. It doesn't need to be fancy. It just needs to include...

- A description of each of your small reports as they are sold individually, along with a link to their respective web sites.

- A description of your "package" offer with a link to its site.

- A listing of your free content available (I.E. The ezine articles you've been writing, etc.) with applicable links to their locations.

- A list to join (I.E. Your newsletter) to receive regular emails from you.

Now, before we move on to phase #5, let me share one more item that I want to mention separately because of the profound effect it can have on your business, especially as it pertains to your portal site.

Here it is –

Create a "mini-course" to give away which is used to promote EACH of your small reports AND your package.

Now that you've got several different "offers" (I.E. Individual reports and your package) it's important that you effectively market them to prospective buyers.

One of the <u>easiest ways</u> to do this is to create a mini-course (A series of related email messages sent out at predetermined intervals through an autoresponder service) that you give away at your portal site.

Each of the lessons in this mini-course would promote an individual report and then in the final lesson of the mini-

```
course you can promote the entire
package.
```

A quick way to create a mini-course is to simply use the existing ezine and blog articles that you've already written. That's fine to begin with. You can always create a brand new mini-course specifically designed for your portal site at a later date.

By adding this mini-course to your portal site, you'll accomplish some very important things to your business...

% **You'll be able to build a list**, which is an invaluable asset to your business as you start, sustain and strengthen relationships with subscribers.

% **You'll be able to automatically promote everything** you offer from one streamlined system.

% **You'll be able to establish your name recognition and build a "presence" online** by regularly contacting your subscribers with each installment of the mini-course.

% **You'll be able to add more messages to the sequence long-term** to promote your new reports as you release them, as well as other people's products and services as an affiliate.

There are many reasons why it's a good idea to have this mini-course. The bottom line is this: it will make you money.

Enough said.

Get your portal site in the works at this phase, along with a mini-course that promotes everything you offer to this point. Then, it's time to continue advancing your business...

Phase #5
Convert Individual Reports Into Featured Products By Developing "Kits"

At this point in your business growth, it's time to begin further developing your individual small reports into feature-length products. This will allow you to sell them at a considerably higher price.

So, the phase here is simply this –

***One at a time, convert each of your existing small
reports into larger products to be sold at higher
prices.***

Now, there are a lot of different ways to do this that we could talk about, but what I want to mention to you is the idea of creating "kits" from your existing small reports.

There are three "Kit Kreators™" that you can use to develop a small report into a premium-priced product.

Let's spend a few minutes talking about them...

Kit Kreator™ #1:
<u>CREATE</u> 3-5 Simple, But Strategic Supplements.

One of the things that separates small reports from full-size products is the inclusion of related supplements. Whether these are marketed as "*bonuses*" or "*accessories*" or "*modules*", the point is the same: by adding more "stuff", you raise the perceived value which allows you to increase your price.

> Now, let me be clear, I'm not talking about throwing in a bunch of cheap ebooks or rehashed stuff found all over the place. I'm talking about adding 3-5 valuable supplements that enhance the information being shared in the small report.

Of course, there are numerous ideas for creating these supplements. If you'd like, I'll be glad to give you some quick ideas to help you better apply this to your own small report:

1) **Checklists**. One of the most popular "supplements" that I've ever created is the "checklist". These are generally 1-3 pages in length and walk the reader through a chronological sequence of action steps to put into practice so they can master whatever was taught in the small report. People love them because they can print them out and follow along, they can use them as a quick overview to follow the process and they can refer back to them over and over again. They are a "must"

for any kind of "how-to" small report.

2) Reference Lists. Another great "supplement" is a "reference list". This would include swipe files, brainstorming ideas, resource rolodex, contacts, categorized vendors, examples, case studies, starters, style sheets, directories, journal entries, etc. Any kind of handy reference list that enhances or expands upon information shared in the small report is a great supplement.

3) Forms. Does your small report require any kind of "form"? Would it be useful for the reader to have some kind of "form" in order to better benefit from your information? Great! Be sure to include one or more in your "kit". Some ideas include: ghostwriter agreements, interview scripts, fill-in-the-blank templates, worksheets, form letters, lesson plans, letterheads, business card layouts, legal documents, evaluation forms, tracking sheets, journal pages, and so forth. Hint: Almost EVERY kind of small report could be enhanced with some kind of "form".

4) Tools. There are occasions when creating a small piece of software or some kind of web-based tool would be a great asset to include in your "kit". Analyze your small report and think about it from the reader's viewpoint. Would they benefit from having a piece of software? Consider these questions...

1. Do readers need to collect data? (Ex. Contacts)

2. Do readers need to track results? (Ex. Weight loss)
3. Do readers need to automate a process? (Ex. Submit articles)
4. Do readers need to search information? (Ex. Recipes)
5. Do readers need to get organized? (Ex. Planner)

If you can answer "yes" to any of these, then I recommend you have a small piece of customized software created to add to your "kit" as a supplement.

Of course, you don't have to create these software programs yourself. You can hire someone at http://www.Elance.com or http://www.odesk.com to do this for you. You can get very simple software programs developed for $200-$300, which is a no-brainer when it comes to adding value (and ultimately increasing orders and profits!) to your "kit". It will pay for itself in no time.

5) **Interaction**. The final one adds a tremendous amount of value. Offer some kind of interaction to the customer as a supplement to your small report.

It could be a free member's forum to discuss ideas, personalized coaching from you, access to an inner circle, a subscription to a "customers only" newsletter, the ability to ask you questions anytime they want, a critique, or any of a dozen other similar ideas.

I offer coaching with many of my different packages, you may choose to do the same.

If you offer some kind of exclusive access where the customer can interact with others and / or yourself as it relates to helping them achieve the results they want from your small report, you've got a winner!

So, that's the first of three "Kit Kreators™" that I want to mention. Create 3-5 simple, but strategic supplements to add to your small report to make it bigger and better.

Kit Kreator™ #2:
CONVERT Portions Of Content Into Audio or Video.

That is, record yourself reading the small report and offer it as a downloadable audio file for your customers. Many, many, many people like to listen to information on their Ipods® or CD player while on the way to work, exercising or just relaxing.

They'd rather HEAR it than READ it.

And – let's face it – audio has a much higher perceived value than text. It always has and it always will. It just "sounds" more expensive. ☺

So, I recommend that you convert your content into audio at a minimum and allow your customers to download it (along with the original report in PDF format) to their computers.

> Sidebar: There are plenty of tutorials
> on how to create downloadable audio files
> available online ranging from free ones
> to low-cost products to premium-priced
> courses. You can search
> http://www.Google.com for more
> information. A good audio-recording tool
> is available at
> http://audacity.sourceforge.net/.

Now, there is also "video" to consider. If there are portions of your content that could be enhanced by a video demonstration, then that's another good idea for adding value to your "kit". Again, you can search or ask for information on how to make downloadable video files.

I've been using downloadable audio and video files as a part of many of my courses for several years now and they always are a huge hit.

Instant value added.

Okay, one more "Kit Kreator™" that I want to talk about before moving on the next "phase"…

Kit Kreator™ #3:
COMBINE Your Small Report With Other Information.

Obviously, if you want to increase your price, you're probably gonna have to increase your information. That is, you'll need to ADD MORE content to your small report to make it a larger work.

While there isn't any real "rule" to govern "how much more" content you need to add, I usually recommend at least 30 pages with an optimum being 50-75 pages.

Don't worry – it really isn't that difficult to take a 10 page report and convert it into 50 pages. Really, it isn't. I promise. ☺

⇒ You can add more content by expanding on each of the existing points you've made in your small report as you explain them in greater detail.

⇒ You can add more content by providing more examples, case studies and ideas for each of the existing points to better illustrate them.

⇒ You an add more content by providing extra points in addition to the ones already shared in the small report.

⇒ You can add more content by introducing related topics and thoroughly explaining them as they fit with your existing content.

⇒ You can add more content by offering "advanced" ideas for those wishing to "graduate" to a greater degree of knowledge or skill as it relates to your small report topic.

⇒ You can add more content by using "padders" such as quotes, charts, screenshots, stories, statistics, research, etc.

⇒ You can add more content by using existing content from other people such as articles, excerpts, interviews, etc. – with their permission, of course.

⇒ You can add more content by asking for questions related to your small report that you answer in great detail as additional information.

⇒ You can add more content by introducing potential problems and offering suggestions on how to prevent and / or overcome these obstacles.

I've just given you 9 quick suggestions on what you can do in order to add more content to your small report. I'm going to give you a 10th one in just a moment after I explain something here.

I want you to think about some of your additional content in terms of a *"part 2"* of your existing small report. Now, the easiest way to offer a part 2 of any product is to use the *"basic to advanced"* model.

Marketing Exhibit™: "Basic to Advanced" Model

If you use the *"Basic to Advanced"* model, then your initial small report would be *"basic"* information, focusing on the beginner level and laying the fundamentals of the topic.

Such as *"A Beginner's Guide to Chess".*

Your part 2 – this additional content - would be at an "advanced" level, sharing information for those who are already experienced (or those who plan to be!)

---

and want something for their advanced state of knowledge, training or experience.

Such as *"Advanced Chess Strategies."*

And it doesn't have to be just based on basic and advanced **skill**, remember to focus on basic and advanced **knowledge** such as:

> "7 Must-See Sights in Orlando" has nothing to do with skill, but could easily be advanced in knowledge by, "7 More Must-See Sights in Orlando." "7 Ways to Cut Travel Costs" could easily be followed up with "7 More Ways to Cut Travel Costs."

You should always have "part 2" information to include as you grow your existing small report into a full-size premium product.

Now, you may not have noticed it, but I've just illustrated the "10th" way you can add content to your special report and that is to ***"recycle portions of your existing content"***.

While you don't want to overdo this, taking excerpts of your existing materials (other small reports, interviews, articles, newsletter issues, forum posts, blog posts, etc.) is a great way to quickly add more content to a special report.

Note: Selling information is a billion dollar business and you have made a great decision in learning this information. Once you get this down, you will be able to write, implement and reap the fruits of your labor for years to come.

Simply repeat this process of converting your small reports into full-length products for EACH of your existing small reports. My recommendation would be to work on ONE conversion each month. That's gonna translate into a huge boost in your business profit!

Okay, now we're really starting to get somewhere with your information business.

But, it gets even better as we move into the final phase...

Phase #6
Use Existing Reports As The Basis
For Premium Content

When you arrive at this final "*phase*", you'll already have a thriving information business, so congratulations on that.

But, that's **not the pinnacle**.

The pinnacle is located at the top of "*Mt. High-Ticket Product*". ☺ Those that climb to the very top are a select few. They are in a group by themselves and they usually make an awful lot of money.

Ready to begin that climb?

Good, because the way you do it is quite clear: *"use existing reports as the basis for premium content"*. In other words, you continue evolving what you've done thus far into the apex of information product business as you develop premium content to offer.

The Big-3 Of "Premium Content" that you want to work towards are...

Premium Content #1: Physical Products. You've undoubtedly seen them before: products consisting of 3-ring notebooks, spiral binders, CDs, DVDs and so forth. These are "physical" products and they command a premium price.

The point is this -

There are much higher profit margins in delivering content in formats <u>other than ebooks</u>.

What has a higher perceived value ... an eBook or a package of notebooks and CDs?

- It's an easy way to increase the perceived value of your product which allows you to...

- Increase the price you charge for your product which allows you to...

- Increase the amount of profit you actually deposit into your account, which is what we're all after.

Now, there are a lot of different options for delivering content in ways other than an eBook that you could offer. Things like...

- Videos
- Printed manuals
- 3-ring binders
- Complete toolkits
- Membership sites
- Webinars
- Teleseminars
- eClasses
- Workshops
- And so forth.

Obviously, we don't have time to cover them all in-depth in this session.

Basically, I just want you to realize that you have options other than eBooks for delivering your content that are potentially much more profitable.

I do want to give you a quick idea that is super simple to implement that can easily double the value of your product, easily double the price you charge for your product.

Easy Way to Double The Price Of Your Product

If you don't want to go to a lot of extra work in creating a different format for your product, then you can at least record yourself reading the entire product and then burning it to a CD that you ship to your customers.

This is an easy way to double the price of your product that costs only 30-40 cents if you burn a CD and stick it in a jewel case, which can easily be self-funded with a shipping and handling charge.

Many people PREFER to "listen" instead of reading (as I mentioned in an earlier session), especially those who are on the road a lot.

Audio books are some of the most popular items of our time, and since they are so easy to create … why not offer one for your product?

Who wouldn't want to double their profit when it's this easy?

Print out your product and convert it into a spiral bound manual and you've got even greater value added to the package.

See how easy this is?

Extra: Another thing you can do is create a 2nd CD with a PDF transcript of your audio on it – which is basically the original product before you recorded it -, as well as some other related reports, articles, bookmarks and resources to add even more perceived value.

Suddenly you've got a 2 CD set that's more of a toolkit than it is an audio book and again your premium pricing increases with the perceived value. It's all about delivering the same content that you're going to distribute anyway – in a new, premium package that commands a higher price tag.

I mean, why would you want to charge $20 for the same content that you could sell for $40 or even more?

What you need to know is this: Nothing about your effort in producing sales is going to change regardless of how much you charge for your product.

- The effort that you take to generate traffic is the same.

- The effort that you take to secure customers is the same.

- The effort that you take to make the sale is the same.

Why not make more money doing what you're going to do anyway?

And, really, there are a couple of additional benefits that are worth mentioning here.

Benefit #1: With a higher profit margin you can raise your visitor value which means you can actually pay more to generate leads, giving you yet another advantage over those who are competing against you.

Benefit #2: And, as we've talked about earlier, by offering a product that sells for a higher price, you are more likely to attract affiliates and joint venture partners to promote your offer for you. If your competition is selling a product for $20 that pays out 50% and you're selling an equally as good product that converts well for $40 that pays out 50%, which one do you think affiliates are going to devote their time and effort to promoting? They are obviously out to make the most money they can make, so you again gain the advantage.

> One more thing I want to mention before we move on. If you have a physical product like a CD or a workbook or something, you can actually charge a shipping and handling fee that covers the cost of duplication, so there isn't any more expense than there would be if it was a digital product.

It's just a no-brainer in my book. It just makes sense and it just makes more money.

Premium Content #2: Live Events. These would consist of workshops, webinars, teleseminars or even e-coaching. Again, we're talking about packaging your content in higher-quality formats.

Look at the differences here just to illustrate why this is such a big money generator...

⇒ You can offer a 4-chapter product that might sell for $47.00 with some bonuses and other "supplements" that we talked about earlier.

⇒ You can tweak that content just a bit to make it interactive, offer it as a 4-week e-coaching program (one chapter per week) where the customer turns in assignments that you grade and personally interact with them and sell basically the same content for 5-10X the price.

The same thing goes for a one or two day workshop, webinar a teleseminar.

People pay a premium price for interaction and personalized attention.

Mark that down. Circle it. Underline it. Make sure it sinks in. It's that important.

The third type of "premium content" that I really consider to be a mandatory part of every information business by phase #6 is...

Premium Content #3: Subscription Sites. Continuity programs where members pay you a recurring fee (either monthly, quarterly or yearly) is a must as far as providing incredible streams of extra income.

I've seen and been part of some of the most successful internet marketing subscription sites ever, so I know what I'm talking about here.

> Sidebar: I've seen membership sites with over 2000 members (some paying as high as $7,000 annually) in them at any one time – that's a whopping million's in annual revenue from ONE site! That's just ONE part of their business.

So, that's why it's so important that you consider putting together a subscription site where you create residual income for yourself.

The simplest way to do this is to setup a subscription site where you offer ONE new "small report" per month related to your topic of expertise.

Record it as an audio and offer it as an "audio newsletter" like I do if you want.

The important thing is this: Over a period of time you'll add a huge chunk of profit to your bottom line as more and more members join and remain active for months and even years to come.

Now, with the typical membership site you offer new content "forever," and your members pay a monthly fee to receive this content "forever." Sounds good in theory, right?

Problem is, there tends to be a high turnover rate on these types of sites. That means in order to keep your income up, you need to keep finding more and more members to replace the ones who're dropping out. Don't get me wrong – this isn't a bad business model. I see kit used all the time. Countless others use it. It is profitable when you have the right offer.

However, there is another membership site solution: the FTM, or fixed-term membership site.

The idea here is that instead of having your membership go on indefinitely, you provide new content (and your subscribers pay a monthly fee) for a fixed-term, such as three months, six months, twelve months or some other pre-determined interval.

The reason this works so well to help boost retention rates is because your members see an end goal in mind. No one likes to quit early when the training is only going to last for a set number of months. This is especially true if you're providing sequential training (Step 1 this month, Step 2 next month, etc), because members want to complete their training.

So, for example, perhaps in a typical membership site that goes on indefinitely, you tend to lose a lot of members around the fourth month. You can easily get those people to stay on and pay for several extra months simply by setting up your site as a fixed-term membership site. And, of course, not only do you get money on front end from membership fees, but you also get backend profits from additional offers you make to your members.

Which brings us to another point...

Creating High-Ticket Offers

As mentioned before, it takes the same effort to get traffic and make sales to your low-priced items as it does to your high-priced items, so it's really in your best interest to create high-ticket (premium) products. These premium offers include home study courses, advanced courses, live courses or personal-interaction such as coaching.

What I've noticed, however, is that a lot of people think they don't know enough to create a high-ticket offer. They can't imagine creating something that they sell for $97, $297 or more.

If you think that way, let me tell you right now that you... yes, YOU... can create a high-ticket offer this week. I'm not kidding. I know this because I've done it myself, and have seen countless others create high-ticket products in as little as 48 hours.

Now, one way to do this is to create a coaching offer. Instead of putting your product purely into text form, you can break it up into modules that you offer alongside live one-on-one coaching.

For example, if your product teaches people how to lose weight, then you can offer live coaching where you help people choose the best diet plan for them as well as helping them develop an exercise program.

Or let's say you have a car-restoration product. You can let your customers ask you five questions about any part of the process related to restoring their classic Camaro (or whatever). To add even more value, you could video record your answers in your garage while using your own classic car as a demo. People would likely pay a lot of money to see you tweak some engine part of install a headliner on video.

So, again, adding personal interaction (coaching) is always a great way to create a high-ticket offer.

However, another way to create a high-ticket offer is by creating a premium product. Sometimes this is an advanced product. In other cases, it might just be a product with a high perceived value.

Now, there's one other slick profit strategy I'd like to share with you...

A Clever Profit Strategy

You have two goals for your products:

> 1. To get a nice profit for every product you sell. For example, if a product sells just as well at $15 as it does at $7, then obviously you want to sell it at the higher price because you get more profit on every sale.

> 2. To get your product into as many peoples' hands as possible. The more customers and readers you have, the more people you have seeing the offers inside your report, clicking on them, and making backend profits for you.

So, here's an idea to maximize your profit per sale while also increasing the number of people who read your report: license your products.

By licensing, I mean that you give other marketers the rights to resell your reports. You sell these licenses for a one-time fee, and in exchange your licensees have the right to resell the product at any price they choose, keep all the profits and of course keep their own customer list.

Here's what you get:

> 1. Licensing fees. You can roughly sell the license to a product for five to ten times its base price. So if you're currently selling a product for $20, you can sell resell rights licenses for that product for $100 to $200. (And you can sell as many licenses as you want –although if you set a lower limit on licenses, people will pay more for the license because they don't have as much competition in the market.)

2. More backend profits. Imagine if you had 10, 20, 50 or more marketers all selling your product. Each of these marketers could sell your product to dozens or perhaps hundreds of new customers. Thus you'll have a far greater reach into the market and thousands of people reading your product who you might not have been able to reach on your own. And each of these readers is a potential newsletter subscriber and/or someone who'll click on the links in your product and purchase additional products. That's pure backend profit for you.

Best of all, you can still keep selling the product on your own even if you license the resell rights to others. Thus you can make money in multiple ways – by selling directly to your customers, by selling the resell rights to other marketers, and by any backend offers you have in your product.

Closing Thoughts

Whew, we have covered just an enormous amount of information.

You've just been handed a tremendous blueprint for getting paid *"With Small Reports"*. I've provided you with an in-depth look at how to build a great business beginning with your first 7-15 page small report all the way to the top of the information product mountain.

The only thing left now is for you to **take action**.

I can tell you what to do and how to do it, *but I can't make you do it.*

That's up to you.

I will close out by reminding you of something that a colleague recently shared with me. He learned this back in his college days and it has **monumentally changed his life**...

There are only two ways to get to the top of an oak tree.

One is to sit on an acorn and **wait**.

The other is to **start climbing**.

See you at the top.

Made in the USA
Middletown, DE
23 February 2019